THE BEST OF THE VILLANS
ASTON VILLA
A-Z

Written by Simon Goodyear

First published in the UK in 2007
Updated and reprinted in 2021

ISBN: 978 1 78281 497 9

© G2 Entertainment Ltd 2021 · www.G2ent.co.uk

Printed and bound printed in Europe

INTRODUCTION

It all started by chance really, shortly after my father, a life-long Aston Villa and England fan and author, passed away in the autumn of 2008. While searching through my father's house, I discovered a scruffy, old plastic bag with what appeared to be a tee-shirt in it.

On closer inspection, I discovered it was an old England football shirt with a number '9' on the back. Not knowing who this 1960s' football shirt belonged to, I later discovered a host of old photos and identified the person as the late Gerry Hitchens. Putting two and two together, I assumed the England shirt also belonged to the ex-Aston Villa, Inter Milan, and England legend who sadly died in 1983. Indeed, it did. What was my father doing with these historical items? Little did I know back then just what treasure I'd discovered and how it would change my life, but it was all good.

It didn't take long for me to contact the Hitchens family, and a few weeks later I returned the photos and the England shirt to the rightful home. However, it wasn't by coincidence that the shirt was in my father's possession; my father was in fact a friend of the Hitchens family, and was in the process of trying to get the shirt displayed in a museum.

In the meantime, I had gained the permission of the family to write Gerry's long-awaited biography. Not having any experience in writing, I set about the task of trying to fill a book with the memories of his family and information taken from newspaper articles, which had been compiled by my father. It could be said that I went into it 'blind', but no more than six months later, and after many trips to North Wales to interview Gerry's widow, Meriel, and eldest son, Marcus, a book was published called, 'The Gerry Hitchens Story: From Mine to Milan'. The rest, as they say, is history.

Much publicity was secured from the publication of the book (and the subsequent discovery of rare 8mm cine film shot by Gerry Hitchens during the 1962 World Cup in Chile), including appearances on the BBC, Sky Sports, and talkSPORT radio, as well as a host of local and national radio shows and newspapers, it did not take long for me to acquire a taste and passion for writing.

Incidentally, that England shirt is now being displayed in the FA Football Museum in Manchester.

In the years that followed, I've written more books, and my latest books document the life stories of football legends Peter Withe (2017) and Brian Little (2018), and a new biography about Aston Villa captain, Jack Grealish (2021).

This book represents a taste of this great club in the format of an A to Z, documenting some great players, managers, owners and some interesting facts about Aston Villa FC.

Simon Goodyear

ACKNOWLEDGMENTS

I would like to thank Jules Gammond and G2 Books for the opportunity to compile this book about all things Aston Villa.

A thank you also goes to fellow Villa fan, radio presenter and good friend of mine, Jonny Gould for his time and effort in sense-checking the manuscript before it went to be edited. Thank you, Jonny.

I would also like to thank my old friend, Aston Villa historian and fellow author, Rob Bishop for his time scouring over the facts for me.

During the writing of this book, the following references were used from the internet:

and James Constant

AVFC.co.uk

Aston Villa: A Complete Record by Rob Bishop & Frank Holt

ALSO BY THE AUTHOR

Gerry Hitchens: From Mine to Milan

Bobby Thomson: The Real Bobby Dazzler

La Storia di Gerry Hitchens (Italian edition)

The Harry Moseley Story - Making It Happen

Memories Made in Aston

Peter Withe: All for the Love of the Game

Cherno Samba: Still in the Game

Brian Little: A Little is Enough

Jack Grealish: Super Jack
Britain's First £100m Player

FOREWORD BY
PETER WITHE

I joined Aston Villa FC in May 1980 and it broke
a dream I had about joining this great club many years
before. However, I had the opportunity to join my
boyhood team in Everton shortly beforehand but chose
Villa instead and that speaks volumes in the faith I had
in the manager, Ron Saunders. We both shared the
same goal, and that was to be successful and to win
trophies - and that was exactly what happened.

I had five years of playing at the club - the longest period
in my football playing career, and another five years on the
management side and that in itself speaks volumes of what
the club meant to me and my family.

The finest moment in a Villa shirt for me, was of
course 'that goal' in Rotterdam on the 26th May 1982.
If I remember rightly, We were doing OK for the first hour.
I was in the middle of the pitch battling for the ball and
I knocked it out to Gary Williams, who then played in Gary
Shaw. Shawy turned inside from the left, Tony Morley
made a run and Shawy looked up and played him in. All
of a sudden, Tony was in a wide position facing Dremmler,
jinking in and out, he managed to get to the touchline.

There was one occasion during the game that I was being
marked by Klaus Augenthaler so I did my usual, which was
to drift off him into space as he followed the ball, but I just
walked towards the path of the ball to see what he would
do. Augenthaler followed me and started to drift to the
near post, just the place I wanted him to be. I peeled off
him, positioned in the middle of the goal. Tony drilled the
ball across the box and in my head everything was
happening in slow motion.

I was thinking, 'We've practised this move a hundred times
...now finish it.' All I had to do was to make good contact
with the ball with my right foot and it was in the back of
the net. As the ball came towards me, it hit a divot in the
penalty area. It bobbled on the pitch and hit the top of my
foot and hit the post before it went into the back of the net.

I wish I could say it was a 35-yard screamer that hit the net so hard it burst the netting, but everyone would know I was lying. It probably wasn't the most beautiful goal I ever scored but I can't remember one I've cherished more. A lot of people said (and still say to this day) that the ball came off my shin but that's a load of rubbish - it definitely came off the top of my foot. If it wasn't for the divot, I'd have had a clean strike at it and I would have drilled it into the net.

The scoreboard read: FC Bayern 0, Aston Villa 1

My momentum carried me forward and I ended up in the back of the net with the ball. I couldn't get out of the goal net for a few seconds, and I remember grabbing hold of the net looking at all the Villa fans cheering in front of me. By the time I managed to untangle myself, Shawy had already got to me, then Gordon came flying in, dived on top of me and shouted, to me and wrestled me to the ground. After a few minutes of celebrating the goal, it was backs-to-the-wall stuff for the next 23 minutes but it was enough to see us through.

PW9 November 2021.

PETER SCORES
THE WINNING GOAL
IN THE 1982
EUROPEAN CUP FINAL
VS BAYERN MUNICH

ACORNS

Aston Villa Football Club has supported the Acorns charity since 2006 and has a long-standing relationship with them. In the 2008/2009 and 2009/2010 Premier League seasons, Villa teamed up with Acorns and displayed their logo adorning the club's shirts and became the first Premier League club to donate their lucrative shirt sponsorship deal to the charitable cause.

JOHN CAREW
MARTIN LAURSEN,,
ASHLEY YOUNG AND
NIGEL REO COKER
MODEL THE NEW KITS
WITH CHILDREN FROM
THE ACORNS CHARITY

Acorns Children's Hospice was also one of the club's official Charity Partners for the 2019/2020 and 2020/2021 seasons. The partnership aimed to raise awareness of Acorns work caring for children and families across Birmingham and the West Midlands.

Over the years, Aston Villa players have also taken the time to visit the children and families who use Acorns, bringing smiles to their faces and those of their hard-working staff.

Gabriel Agbonlahor gave his footballing life to Villa and is the club's highest Premier League goal scorer, beating the previous total of Dwight Yorke (who also played for Villa before the Premier League started).

He joined Villa as a youth and made his way through the ranks, making a name for himself as a prolific scorer - including 40 in one season for the youth team, before being handed his debut by David O'Leary in March 2006.

Villa were struggling at the time and were on the receiving end of a 4-1 drubbing by Everton, although Agbonlahor scored a stunning goal on his debut. He made two more starting appearances that season before really making his presence felt during Martin O'Neill's first campaign in charge.

AGBONLAHOR

Under O'Neill he was a regular in the side and chipped in with his fair share of goals while his blistering pace also set up chances for team-mates. His form was recognised by England in 2008 when he earned three caps over the next 12 months but failed to score in any of his appearances.

A firm favourite with the Villa fans he became club captain for a while at the start of the 2015/2016 season by Tim Sherwood but was dropped from the starting line-up by the incoming manager, Rémi Garde during his short spell in the season.

GABRIEL CELEBRATES SCORING AT THE STADIUM OF LIGHT, 14 MARCH 2015

**LEFT:
GABBY IN PREMIERSHIP ACTION VS SPURS 14 OCTOBER 2006**

ACTIVE SEASONS:	2005/2006 to 2017/2018
APPEARANCES:	391
GOALS:	88

AITKEN

Charlie Aitken holds the record for the most league appearances for Aston Villa. The left-back appeared in 561 league games for the club between April 1961 and May 1976, over a staggering 17 seasons, and played in 660 games overall.

The Scot was born in Edinburgh on 1 May 1942 and began his career with Gorsebridge Juniors and Edinburgh Thistle before his talents took him to Aston Villa. Over the years, Aitken progressed through the reserves and made his first team debut against Sheffield Wednesday in 1961 where his staunch performance as left-back saw him cement his position as a vital part of the defence.

Aitken was part of the Third Division championship winning side in 1972 and had previously won two League Cup runners-up medals (1963 and 1971) before being on the winning side in 1975 (that same year he was voted the Midland Footballer of the Year).

With his dedication and loyalty to the club, Aitken was a successful captain for the first team and his final league match for Villa was, ironically against Sheffield Wednesday, just as his first had been.

He left Villa Park for the other side of the Atlantic where he joined New York Cosmos to play alongside the legendary Pelé. Aitken had been capped once by Scotland in 1961 - 1962 and won two caps in the Under-23s the following season.

ACTIVE SEASONS:	1960/1961 to 1975/1976
APPEARANCES:	660
GOALS:	16

ANGEL

Juan Pablo Ángel became Villa's record signing in January 2001, signed from Club Atlético River Plate for £9.5m. The striker began his illustrious career with Atlético Nacional in Medellín, Colombia and then he was sold to River Plate in Argentina before signing for Villa.

After six years at the club, it was announced in April 2007 that the Colombian footballer would be playing Major League Soccer (MLS) in the United States when he transferred to Red Bull New York.

When he signed for Aston Villa, Ángel took some time to settle in, but the shaky start wasn't enough to dampen the enthusiastic fans and convinced the Chairman and owner, Doug Ellis that he had done the right thing in paying such an enormous fee for the young player.

Ángel then scored 16 goals in his first full season (in all competitions) and became the club's top scorer during the 2003/2004 season with 23 goals (in all competitions). He finally became a favourite with the fans, however, he lost some of his magnetic form during the following three seasons when he only managed to find the back of the net on 19 occasions.

During his time with the club, Ángel managed 62 goals in 205 games across all competitions - only two players have scored more goals for Villa in recent times - Dwight Yorke and Gabby Agbonlahor.

PABLO IN ACTION AT WIGAN ATHLETIC, 19 NOVEMBER 2006

ACTIVE SEASONS:	2000/2001 to 2016/2007
APPEARANCES:	205
GOALS:	62

A JUBILANT DALIAN AFTER
HIS GOAL OF THE SEASON
STRIKE VS WIMBLEDON

ATKINSON DALIAN

Dalian Atkinson joined Aston Villa for £1.6m in July 1991 from Real Sociedad and became one half of another impressive partnership, playing alongside Dean Saunders, who arrived from Liverpool a year after Atkinson arrived at Villa Park. The partnership was broken up in 1995 when both players were sold to Turkish clubs; Saunders to Galatasaray and Atkinson to Fenerbahçe SK for £1.7m.

Atkinson is probably most often remembered for his magnificent solo goal against Wimbledon in a 3-2 away win on 3 October 1992, which won Match of the Day's Goal of the Season award in the first season of the new FA Premier League, when Villa finished runners-up to Manchester United. Starting deep in the Aston Villa half of the pitch with a one-touch trap from a lofted ball that immediately took him away from a defending player, Atkinson then skipped past two more Wimbledon players and, pausing briefly as he reached the edge of the opposition penalty area, produced a delicately arched chip-shot that floated over the rushing goalkeeper. It was a magnificent goal, and one that will be long remembered by Villa fans.

Atkinson had the distinction of scoring Villa's first Premier League goal, when he scored their late equaliser in a 1-1 draw at Ipswich on the opening day of the 1992/1993 season.

Atkinson is also remembered by Aston Villa fans for his goal in the 1994 League Cup final win against Manchester United at Wembley, and that he scored twice in the semi-finals against Tranmere Rovers (once in the first leg and once in the second). In fact, that goal in the first-leg 3-1 defeat at Tranmere gave Villa a lifeline to take back to Villa Park in the second leg.

Atkinson missed Villa's departure for a 1994 pre-season tour of South Africa because of what was described as "personal problems." When Ron Atkinson left and was replaced as manager by Brian Little, he fell out of favour.

In July 1995, Atkinson arrived in Istanbul to agree a deal with Fenerbahçe S.K. but failed to settle in Turkey and had loan spells with Metz and Manchester City. Atkinson ended his career with stints in Saudi Arabia and South Korea, finally retiring as a player in 2001.

Atkinson sadly died on 15 August 2016 after being lasered by police near his father's house in Trench, Telford.

DALIAN CELEBRATES SCORING AGAINST THE RED DEVILS IN THE 1994 COCA COLA CUP FINAL

ACTIVE SEASONS:	1991/1992 to 1994/1995
APPEARANCES:	114
GOALS:	36

BACHE

Joe Bache began his career with Bewdley Victoria before joining Stourbridge FC. He joined Aston Villa for a £100 transfer fee in December 1900 as a 20-year-old. He later became the Villa captain and scored 167 goals in 431 league appearances.

Bache was said to be a cultured inside-forward and also played in midfield and as a left-winger during his 15 years with Villa, which included a spell as captain, succeeding Howard Spencer.

During his Villa career, he picked up two FA Cup winners' medals (1903 and 1913) and a League Championship medal (1910). Bache played for England seven times between 1903 and 1911.

He later made a war-time guest appearance with Notts County but joined Mid-Rhondda FC as player-manager in August 1920 and then Grimsby Town as player-coach on 20 July 1920 to 1921, where he played in five league matches, scoring once, after which time he became a coach in West Germany for four years, including a spell with Mannheim FC from October 1924. He later returned to Villa to become a coach in 1927.

Bache died aged 80 in November 1960, after becoming a licensee in the Aston area of Birmingham.

ACTIVE SEASONS:	1900/1901 to 1914/1915
APPEARANCES:	474
GOALS:	184

BARRY

If Gareth Barry had been blessed with just a tad more pace, he would no doubt have been heralded as one of the great English midfielders of his generation. As it was, he had a fine career with more than 50 England caps and nearly 700 appearances for several Premier League teams.

Barry began his illustrious Villa career in 1997 having been signed from Brighton and Hove Albion by Brian Little as a trainee and started as a central defender where he made up the back three with Ugo Ehiogu and Gareth Southgate.

GARETH, 1998/99

LEFT:
GARETH CELEBRATES SCORING A PENALTY AGAINST EVERTON, APRIL 2009

He soon found his feet in midfield and over the course of the next decade became club captain and was one of the team's most influential and important players. However, he left, somewhat acrimoniously, for Manchester City in June 2009 for a fee of £15m saying he wanted to play in the Champions League.

After 440 appearances and 52 goals for Villa, Barry ensured that he remained a legend at the club.

ACTIVE SEASONS:	1997/1998 to 2008/2009
APPEARANCES:	440
GOALS:	52

BARTON

The talents of Aston Villa manager Tony Barton were evident for all to see during the 1981/1982 season when the club won the European Cup final just months after he took charge.

Anthony Edward Barton was born on 8 April 1936 in Sutton, Surrey and his love of football began at an early age, and he won five youth caps and a schoolboy cap before his career began as a trainee for Fulham. He was loaned to Sutton United before turning professional for Fulham in May 1954. Playing on the outside-right, Barton netted eight goals in 49 appearances for the club before signing for Nottingham Forest in December 1959.

He never found his feet with the club, however, and scored only once in his 22 appearances for Forest and moved to Portsmouth just two years later. It was here that Barton became a player-coach and after 130 appearances and 34 goals, he hung up his boots and retired as a player; however, he came into his own on the coaching staff.

He joined the coaching team at Aston Villa and in 1980 became assistant manager to Ron Saunders. Villa claimed the league title the following year - the first time they had done so in 71 years.

When Saunders unexpectedly resigned in February 1982, the obvious choice to replace him was Barton. He followed the club's success with victory over Bayern Munich in the European Cup in 1982 and the following year took his team to further victory in the European Super Cup. However, league performances were not as impressive and chairman Doug Ellis, "who would not tolerate anything but success" sacked Barton in May 1984.

Barton was replaced by Graham Turner two months later, who like Barton, managed to hold on to his position for two years. in the same month that Turner succeeded Barton, the former Villa manager took over at Northampton Town. The following year, Barton suffered a heart attack and his days with his new club were over. He became assistant manager at Southampton working with Chris Nicholl then became assistant manager at Portsmouth before the sacking of Frank Burrows saw him take the hotseat in February 1991. After much ill health, Tony Barton sadly died of a heart attack on 20 August 1993.

BENTEKE

Christian Benteke quickly became a popular player with the Villa faithful since joining in the summer of 2012 and the Villa fans immediately gave him the nickname, 'Beast', in relation to his muscular physique. In his first two seasons with the club, the burly centre-forward notched a goal every other game in his 60-odd appearances.

He led the line superbly and gave Villa a real presence up top after joining the club from Belgium club, Genk, for £7.9m where he had scored 19 goals in just 37 appearances during the 2011/2012 season. Previously, he started his career with Standard Liège.

In the summer of 2015, Benteke was transferred to Liverpool for £32.5m following Villa's FA Cup Final defeat to Arsenal and spent an uncomfortable season there, scoring 10 goals for the Reds. He was then transferred to Crystal Palace for around £27m at the start of the 2016/2017 season and that is where he remained at the time of writing.

Benteke's international career began at a young age for Belgium, appearing 24 times at youth level before making his senior debut in May 2010 against Bulgaria, after being picked for the squad by his former coach at Kortrijk, Georges Leekens.

He was a regular in the Villa squad during the 2013/2014 season but tragically a freak training ground injury at Villa in April when he ruptured his Achilles meant that he played no part in the 2014 World Cup in Brazil. However, he was part of the Belgium squad in the Euro 2016 championships.

CHRISTIAN CELEBRATES AT THE FINAL WHISTLE AFTER BEATING LIVERPOOL 2-1 IN THE 2015 FA CUP SEMI-FINAL

ACTIVE SEASONS:	2012/2013 to 2014/2105
APPEARANCES:	101
GOALS:	49

BODYMOOR HEATH

Aston Villa's training Ground at Bodymoor Heath in North Warwickshire has been undergoing a major redevelopment since 2007. In 2021 it is now one of the finest and most modern training grounds in Europe, if not the world, and it's still being improved. It is a million mile away from when it was first opened.

The land situated near the M42 motorway was originally bought from a local farmer by the then Villa chairman, Doug Ellis in the early 1970s and the complex was considered 'state of the art' when it first opened.

Many players have homes in the area so they can be close to the ground, located in a rural and desirable part of Warwickshire.

Villa have been trying to modernise the facilities for many years but were repeatedly hindered by planning restrictions until plans were announced in November 2005 to update Bodymoor Heath. However, when Randy Lerner took over the ownership of the club in September 2006, the original plans were upgraded and so was the cost, from £8m to £13m and the redevelopment was finally opened in May 2007.

The facility then boasted four pitches, new changing rooms and a health and fitness suite to rival any in the world at that time. The latter included a swimming pool, underwater treadmills as well as hot and cold therapy pools all designed to keep the players fit and speed up their return from any injury suffered. The second phase of the development comprised the construction of dining and conference rooms together with offices.

In March 2019, under the ownership of the current incumbents, Wes Edens and Nassef Sawiris, the club submitted more plans to expand the gym and sports science areas of the training ground, as well as adding a larger match analysis room, and increasing the area used for physical training, which was said to be inspired by the facilities of the NFL team, Minnesota Vikings.

Not only that, but due to the relocation of the southern end of the training ground, due to loss of land caused by the development of HS2, the Academy training ground was also completely redeveloped, and a 500-seater 'mini-stadium' was constructed, so that the Under-23 team could play at Bodymoor Heath, instead of Villa Park.

That phase of the redevelopment cost an estimated £20m and continued throughout 2020, partly funded by HS2 compensation. It was officially opened by HRH Prince William on 4th May 2021.

THE DUKE OF CAMBRIDGE SPEAKS TO ASTON VILLA PLAYERS DURING THE OFFICIAL OPENING OF VILLA'S HIGH PERFORMANCE CENTRE AT BODYMOOR HEATH

PAUL BIRCH, 1987/88

BIRCHY

Paul Birch (Birchy) began his career in the Aston Villa youth system, becoming a regular first-team player during the 1983/1984 season after making his league debut on 29 August 1983 in a 1-0 win at home to Sunderland. His first-team debut had come earlier that year when he replaced Gary Shaw for the final twelve minutes of the European Super Cup victory at home to Barcelona.

During Villa's decline in the mid-1980s he was the mainstay of their midfield, able to play on the right or in the centre of midfield and through his tenacious performances became a Holte End favourite. He was part of the Villa side that were relegated in 1987, but helped them win promotion under new manager Graham Taylor a year later. He came close to winning a league title medal in 1990, but Villa were beaten into second place by Liverpool.

However, when Jozef Vengloš became Villa manager at the start of the 1990/1991 season Birch found himself out of the team and was sold to local rival Wolverhampton Wanderers who were in Division Two in January 1991, for £400,000 where he joined up with former manager Graham Turner (who had been at Villa Park from 1984 to 1986).

He had served Aston Villa for over 10 years and was awarded a testimonial by the club in August 1991.

Birch stayed at Wolves for five years as the club (unsuccessfully) tried to break into the Premier League. He was almost an ever-present under Graham Turner but found regular appearances harder to come by after Wolves appointed another former manager of his, Graham Taylor.

He was finally released by Wolves in May 1996, where he finished his career with a season at both Doncaster Rovers and Exeter City before retiring from professional football and joining Halesowen Town in the Southern Premier League.

He had a spell as a postman before joining the coaching staff at Forest Green Rovers in 2001, working under his former Villa teammate Nigel Spink and remained with the club after Spink was sacked. He left Rovers in August 2003 to take up a role coaching the youth teams at Birmingham City, where Spink was goalkeeper coach.

Sadly, in May 2008, it was revealed he was suffering from bone cancer and later died on 2 February 2009 at the Good Hope Hospital in Sutton Coldfield.

Even to this day, the name of Paul Birch lives in the memory of Villa fans, and you can still hear his name sung by the faithful fans in the Holte End.

ACTIVE SEASONS:	1983/1984 to 1991/1992
APPEARANCES:	223
GOALS:	250

MARK GATHERS THE BALL ABOVE LIVERPOOL'S ROBBIE FOWLER DURING THE 1996 FA CUP SEMI-FINAL

BELOW:
MARK CELEBRATES WITH DWIGHT YORKE AFTER BEATING LEEDS UNITED IN THE 1996 COCA COLA CUP FINAL

BOZZIE

Born to Croatian parents in Fairfield, New South Wales in Australia on 13 January 1972, Mark Bosnich was a star goalkeeper who became renowned for being one of the best Australian players in history. Despite his reputation as an international goalkeeper, it was Bosnich's time at Aston Villa that firmly established his career while his spells at Manchester United and Chelsea also helped to raise his profile.

It was during the League Cup semi-final in 1994 against Tranmere Rovers that Bosnich is best remembered. It was his exceptional skills that saw the Australian make three stunning penalty saves as Aston Villa beat their opponents in the penalty shoot-out. It set Bosnich on the road to international glory where he went on to make 22 appearances for his country - even scoring a goal with a late penalty in a 13-0 victory over the Solomon Islands.

It all began for 'Bozzie' when he started playing for local team Sydney Croatia in the Australian National Soccer League (A-League) aged just 16, Bosnich travelled to the UK to play initially for Manchester United's youth team on a three-year contract but after only three appearances for the club, he was denied a work permit and was forced to return to his native Australia. However, his ties to the UK were made permanent when he married a UK resident, and he was able to return having been lured by Aston Villa's then boss Ron Atkinson.

After Bosnich's success in that League Cup semi-final, Villa went on to win the final against Manchester United and Bosnich further impressed his club when he played a vital role in the 1996 League Cup which once again saw Villa claim the trophy.

After a total of 228 appearances for Villa, the Australian moved back to Old Trafford in 1999 where he succeeded Peter Schmeichel as the first team goalkeeper. he didn't fare well under Sir Alex Ferguson and moved to Chelsea on a free transfer in 2001. Unfortunately, his life was to spiral downwards and following a bitter marriage break-up he then tested positive for drugs in 2002. In December that year he was charged by the FA for bringing the game into disrepute and was given a nine-month ban. Following a disciplinary hearing that was initially postponed, Bosnich brought a case of unfair dismissal against Chelsea. However, the FA found in favour of the club and Bosnich was left with no job and suffered a bout of depression.

He is now smiling again as a media pundit (based in Australia) offering frequent fascinating observations on the UK sports radio station, talkSPORT.

ACTIVE SEASONS:	1991/1992 to 1998/1999
APPEARANCES:	228
GOALS:	0

CAREW

John Carew started his professional career with Vålerenga in 1997, playing 58 times and scoring 30 goals before being transferred to Rosenborg, where is profile grew, scoring 19 goals in just 17 games.

His big move came in 2000 when he was transferred to Valencia for €8.5m and he helped the Spanish club win two La Liga titles and a loser's medal in the 2001 Champions League Final. Short spells at Roma (on loan), Beşiktaş and Lyon followed, before his big move to the Premier League and to Aston Villa in January 2007 for £3.5m.

JOHN IN PREMIER LEAGUE ACTION AT STAMFORD BRIDGE, MARCH 2010

Carew made his debut for Villa in a 3-1 defeat to Newcastle but scored his first goal in a 1-0 win against West Ham. In the 2007/2008 season, Villa manager Martin O'Neill made Carew his sides first choice striker and a lot was expected of him; however, it took him two months to score his first goal of the that season, in a 2-0 victory against Everton.

His dominant size was always going to incur fear in defenders (and some attention from referees) and he played on his natural characteristics with some success. Though a big player, his ground-play could be troublesome to defences at times.

It was his two goals against local rivals Birmingham City at Villa Park in April 2008 that made the well-travelled Norwegian a folk hero, as Villa went on to win 5-1.

Since that day, the big striker undoubtedly became a huge favourite with the Holte End, whose hymn is still sung to this day: "John Carew, Carew, he's bigger than me and you ...".

During the following season, he formed a pretty formidable partnership with Gabby Agbonlahor as Villa had a run in Europe. However, he made the headlines for the wrong reasons in October 2008 when he was caught in a lap dancing club in Birmingham, the night before a crucial UEFA Cup game against Ajax and was fined two weeks wages by the club.

With the signing of Emile Heskey, Carew failed to hold down a regular place during the 2009/2010 season, but still scored important goals for Villa, including some coming on from the bench. The 2010/2011 season was Carew's last in a Villa shirt, as he found his chances limited, mainly due to the sudden departure of Martin O'Neill on the eve of the new season. The £18m record signing of Darren Bent in January 2011 didn't help and his departure was announced on 27th May 2011.

Short spells at Stoke City and West Ham followed before he retired from playing.

John Carew played at every level for Norway and was capped 91 times, scoring 24 international goals. He is still a firm favourite with the Villa fans and has been seen in the crowd several times with his friend, fellow Villa fan, HRH Prince William.

ACTIVE SEASONS:	2006/2007 to 2010/2011
APPEARANCES:	131
GOALS:	48

COWANS

Gordon 'Sid' Cowans is more than familiar with Aston Villa, having joined the club on three separate occasions as a player alone, and later also as a coach. Cowans first joined Villa as an apprentice in July 1974 when he was just 15 years old and received his first team call-up in 1976 and became a professional on his 18th birthday.

GORDON, 1989/90

The 1976/1977 season saw the young player establish himself as a regular in a Villa side that won the League Cup. The midfielder was renowned for his exceptional two-footed control and his skills on the pitch earned him the 1979/1980 PFA Young Player of the Year. Cowans was stoic in midfield as Villa went on to win the league in 1980/1981 and was a pivotal part of the side which saw Villa gain victory in the European Cup against Bayern Munich a year later.

The following season, Villa reached the quarter-finals of the European Cup trying to defend their title but were disappointed when Juventus knocked them out of the tournament.

There was some consolation, however, when Cowans scored from the rebound following a penalty miss in the victory over Barcelona that brought the European Super Cup to Villa Park in the same season.

By this time, the young midfielder had attracted the attention of England boss Bobby Robson who gave Cowans his first full cap against Wales at Wembley in 1983. However, tragedy struck when he broke his leg in a friendly against Spain which saw him out of action for the whole of the 1983/1984 season. When Graham Taylor took the helm at Villa, Cowans was quickly sold in 1985 to Italian side Bari, a move which left Villa fans devastated by the loss of "Sid".

In his second season for the Italian club, under new manager Enrico Catuzzi, Cowans was more on the pitch than off it as Catuzzi struggled to find a winning formula for his new club. After two years abroad, Cowans made it known he wanted to return to English football and Graham Taylor quickly brought the midfielder 'home' in 1988.

Taylor was then appointed England manager and he picked Cowans to face the Republic of Ireland in a Euro '92 qualifying match. He eventually won 10 caps for England and found the back of the net on two occasions.

Just before the start of the 1991/1992 with Ron Atkinson as Villa manager, he was sold to Blackburn Rovers before returning for his third spell at Villa in 1993, where he stayed for a year and made 11 appearances for the club. He then had spells at several clubs, including Derby, Wolves and Sheffield United before he retired as a player in 1997.

'Sid' was arguably the best all-round Villa player in the clubs' history and will always be remembered with great fondness by Villa fans from every generation. With the 527 appearances he made for Villa, including being ever-present for four seasons between 1979 and 1983, they are great testament to his consistency, especially as he had spells away from the club. In fact, when 'Sid' retired from playing, he started a coaching career, not at Villa, but with Burnley of all places, before moving back to his spiritual home for the fourth time to become youth team coach in 1998 and then as part of Gérard Houllier's first team coaching staff in 2014. He had a couple of short spells taking temporary charge of first team matters, until he finally left Villa in September 2016.

ACTIVE SEASONS:	**1975/1976 to 1993/1994**
APPEARANCES:	527
GOALS:	59

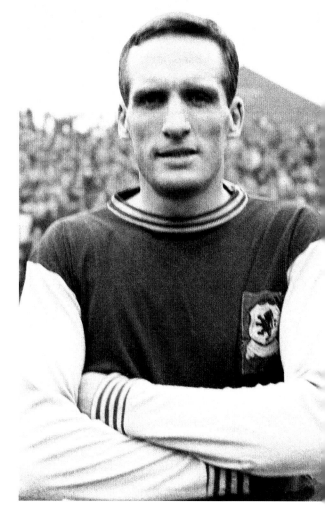

CROWE

Vic Crowe was one of a small number of people who not only played for the Aston Villa but also became their manager; there probably hasn't been a more committed person to the cause of Aston Villa. He was also club captain, which made him a very special person indeed in the history of Aston Villa FC.

Crowe signed for Villa in 1951 after being part of the West Bromwich Albion youth setup and eventually took over at right-half from the departed Danny Blanchflower half-way through the 1954/1955 season and was a regular through the remainder of that season and virtually all of the next nine seasons.

However, he unfortunately missed out on Villa's triumphant FA Cup-winning season (1956/1957) as a result of an injury and his absence gave the opportunity for Stan Crowther to come in and make his mark. Crowe was a regular in the side once Crowther signed for the famous Manchester United side managed by Sir Matt Busby after the devastating Munich air crash.

Although he was seen as a Brummie, Crowe was in fact born in Wales and played for the Welsh national side, eventually becoming their captain as well. He was a member of the Welsh squad that participated in the 1958 World Cup Finals in Sweden and was capped 16 times. He also played for Wales at Villa Park against England in the November 1961.

Crowe was a key member of Villa's promotion-winning side of 1959 - 1960 and then led the Villa in winning the first-ever League Cup in 1961.

On leaving the Villa as a player in 1964, after 351 appearances, he signed for Peterborough United, and then went to the USA, following his former Villa and Wales playing colleague Phil Woosnam in providing expertise to the American soccer team, Atlanta Chiefs, where he played 51 times until returning to Villa as assistant coach in 1969.

Vic was committed the Villa cause; his enthusiasm shone in everything he did whilst with the Villa, and when he took over the managerial role from Tommy Docherty in January 1970 and tackled the job of getting Villa back into the top league from being a Third Division club.

Along the way, he managed the Villa side who lost the League Cup Final against Tottenham Hotspur and eventually saw his side win the Third Division title in 1972. However, it all ended in the club's Centenary year of 1974 when he was sacked after his side finished 14th in Division Two and replaced by Ron Saunders.

Vic Crowe will be remembered at Villa for the aforementioned triumphs indeed, but he also managed the side who beat Pele's great Santos side, albeit in a friendly at Villa Park, and developing the side who won the FA Youth Cup in 1972, a side that produced a number of players who would break through into the first team, the likes of: Brian Little, John Gidman, Jimmy Brown, Tony Betts and Bobby McDonald.

After leaving the managerial role at Villa, he spent two spells managing Portland Timbers in the NASL. He sadly passed away aged 76 after a long illness in January 2009.

ACTIVE SEASONS:	1954/1955 to 1963/1964
APPEARANCES:	351
GOALS:	12

DALEY

Tony Daley joined his hometown club, Aston Villa, as an apprentice at the age of **14** and made his senior debut, aged **17**, on **20 April 1985** in a 2-0 defeat at Southampton. He played for Villa for ten seasons, nine at the highest level, and finished a runner-up in both the league seasons of **1989/1990** and **1992/1993**.

He also played in their victorious 1994 League Cup Final against Manchester United at Wembley and nearly got onto the scoresheet, but his shot hit the post and was rebounded by Dalian Atkinson only for Andrei Kanchelskis to block it with a handball for which he was sent off.

Dean Saunders converted the penalty and put Villa 3-1 ahead, a score-line which formed the final result and gave Villa a fifth League Cup win. Daley collected what would be the only major trophy of his career.

During this period, Daley was capped seven times for England between 1991 and 1992 under former club manager Graham Taylor. He made his full debut as a substitute in a vital 1-1 draw in Poland on 13 November 1991 that saw England qualify for 1992 European Championships.He was subsequently chosen for the squad at the tournament and played in two of England's three games there, but after the tournament he never played for England again.

Daley linked up with Graham Taylor again as he finally left Villa for Wolverhampton Wanderers in July 1994 for £1.25 million, along with his former-Villa teammate, Steve Froggatt, but he was plagued with injuries and was only able to manage 21 appearances for the club in four seasons.

He was signed once more in July 1998 by Graham Taylor, who was Watford manager, on a free transfer. His injury woes continued though, and he struggled to get fit, missing the final months as the club won promotion to the Premier League. He was given a free transfer to newly promoted Division One side, Walsall in June 1999, and after a six-month spell there, he finished his playing career with Conference side Forest Green Rovers, finally hanging up his boots in July 2002.

Daley's perhaps best-known goal came in a First Division game against Everton at Villa Park on 22 October 1988, a spectacular flying volley in a 2-0 win for Villa, the goal quickly, thanks in no small part to the popular football video series 'Goals Galore', became known as 'Daley's Dazzler' and is also remembered for full-back Chris Price (who supplied the cross) having a little celebration all of his own.

ACTIVE SEASONS:	1984/1985 to 1993/1994
APPEARANCES:	290
GOALS:	3

DELANEY

Welsh defender Mark Delaney began his career with Carmarthen in the League of Wales before coming to the attention of Cardiff City manager Frank Burrows. Born in Haverfordwest on 13 May 1976, Delaney joined the 'Bluebirds' on a free transfer on 1 June 1998 and made 35 appearances. Less than a year later, Delaney found himself on the way to Aston Villa in a transfer deal that cost the club £250,000 in March 1999.

The right-back made a good impression at his new club although he spent much of his early days playing for the reserves. Despite repetitive knee injuries, Delaney continued to impress at Villa and played in the 2000 FA Cup Final defeat to Chelsea and then made 39 appearances in the 2001/2002 season where his place in the first-team became firmly established. The result was a four-year contract for the young player who was also proving himself in the Welsh national side - especially in their famous victory over Germany.

Delaney made 36 appearances for Wales, but injury hindered his opportunities in 2002/2003 after Delaney broke his foot and the following season wasn't much better as further injuries saw him remain on the bench. In the end, his knee problem proved so persistent that Delaney retired after more than 150 league games for villa at the age of 31 in 2007.

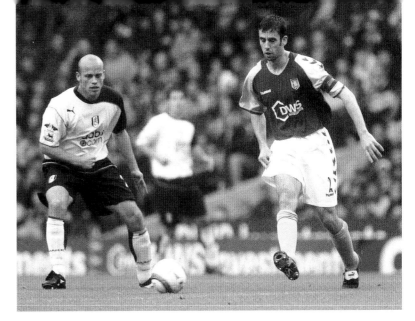

MARK IN ACTION AGAINST FULHAM'S CLAUS JENSEN, OCTOBER 2004

Upon retiring from playing, Delaney remained at Villa as a youth team coach where he has subsequently risen through the ranks. Since the 2015/2016 season, he has been the club's Under-23 coach, overseeing the progression of the top talent from the youth ranks through to the second string and beyond.

On 8th January 2021, Delaney famously took charge of Villa in their FA Cup Third Round tie with Liverpool at Villa Park, due to the absence of first-team coach Dean Smith and his entire backroom team, amid the backdrop of the COVID-19 outbreak at the Bodymoor Heath training ground during that week. Although Delaney didn't manage the first-team on that evening, he did field his Under-23 side; however, the result didn't go his way as Villa went down to Liverpool's first-team by 4-1, although a spectacular equalising goal from Louie Barry on half-time made the game interesting for the first hour.

ACTIVE SEASONS:	1998/1999 to 2006/2007
APPEARANCES:	193
GOALS:	2

DERBY DAY

It isn't surprising for a city the size of Birmingham to have two top-class football clubs that were both formed many years ago when professional football was in its fledgling years. As the UK's second city, Birmingham boasts Aston Villa, formed in 1874 and Birmingham City, established the following year as Small Heath Alliance.

History books record their first clash as being played at Small Heath's Muntz Street ground on 27 September 1879, with the home side winning the match by one disputed goal. It must be said here that the Villa players apparently described the Muntz Street ground as "only suitable for pot-holing", something the modern fans may think about the Blues' current ground at St Andrews.

The 'Second City Derby' started as it was meant to continue - in controversy and banter.

With Villa being founder members of the Football League in 1888, it wasn't until Small Heath joined the newly formed Second Division in 1892 that there was any chance of the two teams meeting in a competitive fixture. Small Heath gained promotion to the top-flight two years later and the intense rivalry between the two clubs began with a 1st September clash at Villa Park to open the 1894/1895 season. The home side won this encounter 2-1 with goals from Steve Smith and Robert Gordon but drew 2-2 in the return game in the October.

The two clubs have been paired once in the FA Cup and that was in the third round of the 1900/01 competition. A goalless draw at Muntz Street was followed by a single goal victory at Villa Park courtesy of centre-forward Billy Garraty (great, great grandfather of Jack Grealish).

However, the Football League Cup (now the EFL Cup) has been a different story with the first meeting of the two clubs in the 1962/1963 Final. On that occasion, the blue half of Birmingham emerged victorious from the encounter, winning the home leg 3-1 before a goalless draw at Villa Park.

Both clubs are generally regarded as each other's most fierce rivals, but haven't always been in the same league, so games have sometimes been in short supply. During the late 1970s and early 1980s, both clubs met regularly in the First Division and there were some memorable fixtures. In Villa's triumphant 1980/1981 season, Villa did the double over Blues as they went on to win the league. However, in the season after Villa won the European Cup (1982/1983 season), Blues beat the Villa by 3-0 at St Andrews.

After those triumphant years for Villa, both clubs went on a decline, and during Villa's 1985/986 relegation season, Blues claimed a 3-0 win at Villa Park.

The sides clashed again in the second round of the 1988/1989 League Cup competition and that time Villa got their revenge with a comprehensive 7-0 thrashing of their neighbours over the two-legged tie. Aston Villa again met Birmingham City in the second round five years later with a similar outcome. A 1-0 score-line in each leg gave Villa the opportunity to progress.

In the Premier League era, the two clubs met twice in the second round of the 1993/1994 League Cup, Villa winning both 1-0 and went on to win the trophy. Birmingham's promotion to the Premier League in 2002 saw the first league derby for 15 years; however, Villa lost on both occasions. Both games were made famous by goalkeeping errors by Villa's 'keeper, Peter Enckelman, and included a goal scored direct from a throw-in by Olof Mellberg. Both games were marred by crowd trouble. In the game at Villa Park in March 2003, the game erupted on the pitch too, with a famous bust-up between Dion Dublin and Robbie Savage, which resulted in Dion Dublin being sent off for head-butting Robbie Savage - and soon became a Villa legend. Later in the game, Villa's Joey Guðjónsson also got sent off for a two-footed tackle.

Other famous games included 3-1 Villa home win when Gary Cahill scored with a superb bicycle kick in front of the Holte End. In April 2008, Villa recorded their biggest win for 40 years over their rivals (5-1). The record books were broken in April 2010 when Villa won their sixth straight league win over Blues, with the next two games being draws.

JACK GREALISH HITS THE WINNER AT ST ANDREW'S, MARCH 2019

Birmingham were relegated from the Premier League in 2011 and haven't been back there since. However, Villa were relegated in 2015 so the second city derby was restored for three seasons while Villa struggled to get back into the Premier League.

The most famous recent meeting took place at St Andrews in March 2019 when a thug ran onto the pitch and attacked Villa captain Jack Grealish. Karma was restored when Jack scored the winning goal.

VILLA'S RECORD AGAINST BIRMINGHAM CITY:

GAMES WON:	57
GAMES DRAWN:	33
GAMES LOST:	38

DIXON

Johnny Dixon was a true Villa legend. He made his way to Villa Park as an amateur in 1944 by writing to the club for a trial and then became a professional just after the World War 2.

Dixon slowly made progress under the direction of manager Alex Massie and gained some prominence during a tour of Norway, when his goal-scoring was noted. However, although by 1949 he had played 55 first-class games and scored 18 goals in the process and wasn't considered to be a first-team regular until the 1949/1950 season, when his Villa career really took off and he became a mainstay of the team, hitting double-figures in terms of goals in seven out of the next nine seasons; in the 1951/1952 season, he scored as many as 28 goals in 43 matches in a season when the Villa finished sixth in the League.

It was a mystery why Dixon never played for England, given his class and goalscoring ability. At the age of 28, Dixon had formed a great partnership with Tommy Thompson, who both played as 'inside-forwards' and he was reaching his peak. The future of the Villa looked as though it was bright, but manager George Martin left early in the season of 1953/1954 and was replaced by ex-Villa player, Eric Houghton.

Dixon was made captain at the age of 32, but Houghton made changes to the side and Dixon lost nearly all of his familiar playing partners as Villa narrowly escaped relegation. The following season was regarded as the climax of Dixon's career as he lifted the FA Cup in 1957, after that famous 2-1 win over Manchester United. It was Villa's first major trophy in 37 years - and a trophy that the Villa have not won since! At the age of 34, the following season was the start of the downturn of Dixon's career, and it wasn't too surprising that he was mainly out through

injury and health problems. Eric Houghton was replaced by Joe Mercer, and Dixon was given one final run during the relegation season of 1958/1959, playing at wing-half, but it was clear that Mercer was looking to re-build.

In the final game of the 1960/1961 season, Joe Mercer brought 37-year-old Dixon on for one last game against Sheffield Wednesday and Villa won 4-1. That game proved to be the last appearance for another Villa legend, Gerry Hitchens, who scored two goals, and Dixon also scored a good goal, following which young boys ran onto the pitch, and the crowd gave him an outstanding ovation on

his return to the centre circle that went on and on until the game was re-started.

Although he retired from playing, Dixon remained on the Villa's staff as a coach until 1967, and then retired from football to concentrate on his business as a shopkeeper of an ironmongers.

ACTIVE SEASONS:	1945/1946 to 1960/1961
APPEARANCES:	430
GOALS:	144

JOHNNY HOLDS
THE FA CUP ALOFT
AFTER HIS TEAM'S
2-1 VICTORY OVER
MANCHESTER UNITED
MAY 1957

EDENS & SAWIRIS

On 20th July 2018 it emerged that an Egyptian company called the **NSWE** group and owned by the Egyptian billionaire **Nassef Sawiris** and the American billionaire **Wes Edens** were to invest in **Aston Villa Football Club.**

They had purchased a controlling 55% stake in the club at a cost of a reported £30m and Sawiris took over the role of executive chairman and Edens taking the role of co-chairman. However, the previous owner, Dr Tony Xia initially remained as another co-chairman. Apparently, the whole deal took nine days to thrash out.

What the Villa fans were most interested in was the wealth of the two new owners. Sawiris was said to have a personal wealth of around £5.2bn, making him the richest Egyptian in the world and Edens, co-owner of the Milwaukee Bucks, a National Basketball Association (NBA) franchise based in Milwaukee, Wisconsin, was estimated to be worth around £1.9bn. Their combined wealth immediately made them the third richest owners in English football.

Christmas had come early to Aston Villa Football Club. What the fans liked most about the new owners, was their intent for the club, which was demonstrated in their first press statement:

"Our goal is to bring sustainable success to the club, building on its rich history while respecting its loyal fan base and unique culture. We understand that we are stewards of Aston Villa on behalf of the fans, and we take that responsibility seriously."

A season after the club had lost the 2018 Championship Play-Off Final against Fulham, Villa returned to Wembley for the 2019 Final, with new owners' intent on gaining promotion back to the Premier League. The club had been transformed from the one they had taken over, which was on the brink of bankruptcy and couldn't even afford to pay outstanding tax bills; the money had run out and Dr Xia couldn't access his assumed wealth from his homeland. In short, it was a shambles.

That final at Wembley on 27th May 2019 ended up in victory as we all know, and a year afterwards and another £126.4m pumped into the club by the owners, Aston Villa FC was almost unrecognisable. Following promotion, just over £156m was invested in 16 new players.

Another huge sum, well over £130m was invested in the following season, including a record-breaking signing of Ollie Watkins from Brentford for £28m.

Fast forward to the summer of 2021, and there was talk of £200m being made available to Villa manager Dean Smith, with £40m rated Argentinian midfielder, Emi Buendia being top of their list. There is now a long-term plan which includes investing heavily season-on-season in players, redeveloping the North Stand and the training ground, as well as projects away from Villa Park in the local community.

No wonder the Villa fans are in heaven, they just love Edens and Sawiris.

JACK GREALISH AND TEAMMATES CELEBRATE WINNING THE 2019 CHAMPIONSHIP PLAY-OFF FINAL

ELLIS

Sir Douglas Herbert Ellis OBE could have been described as controversial and inimitable. Born in Cheshire in January 1924 his early life was particularly difficult; however, despite his disadvantaged childhood, Ellis soon became a successful entrepreneur.

A former footballer himself, having trials with Tranmere Rovers as a youngster, he chose a path in business rather than football and pioneered the package holiday to Spain in the 1960s with his company, Sunflight. His business acumen made him a millionaire by the time he was 40.

He joined the club in 1968 and he carried out his duties as Villa chairman before being replaced in 1975. He remained on the board before being removed in 1979 but was back at the helm in 1982. Ironically, it was during Ellis's brief absence from the club (1979 - 1982), that the team enjoyed unrivalled success and were champions of both the Football League (1981) and the European Cup (1982). Ellis came in for considerable criticism when the club were relegated in 1987, as he sold many players to counter spiralling debts.

Ellis was famously nicknamed "Deadly Doug" by England legend Jimmy Greaves, apparently following a fishing trip when Greaves saw Doug knocking a salmon on the head! Another story was that Greaves used the term after Doug's liking to sacking his managers. In fact, during his tenures as chairman, he had 13 different managers and only two returned any silverware, with Ron Atkinson and Brian Little both bringing home the League Cups in 1994 and 1996 respectively.

In 1996, Ellis owned 47% of Aston Villa and a year later he floated the club on the stock market with a valuation of £126m and he sold a number of shares, reducing his holding to around 39%, and made a few pounds along the way, too. He was reportedly the first chairman to pay himself a salary when it was made legal by the FA for a chairman to do so.

In 2004, at the age of 80, Ellis was diagnosed with Prostate Cancer, and he agreed to relinquish some of his control of the club by appointing a CEO in Bruce Langham, but he only lasted less than a year following a disagreement with Mr Ellis.

Villa supporters always had a love/ hate relationship with Mr Ellis, some alleging the former chairman lacked any ambition to move the club forward in the Premier League era. In August 2006, Mr Ellis finally announced he was selling the club to American billionaire, Randy Lerner in a deal worth around £62.6m, and it signalled a new era for the club. He stood aside when the takeover was completed but part of the deal entitled him to become the club's first President Emeritus (a Life President).

No new owners were going to get rid of 'Deadly Doug' that easily.

In 2005, Ellis was handed an OBE in the New Year Honours list; in March 2012 he was knighted by HM the Queen for his contribution to charity work. Mr Ellis sadly passed away aged 94 on 11th October 2018.

His legacy remains at Villa Park in the form of the former Witton Lane Stand, which he named after himself in the 1990s - 'The Doug Ellis Stand'.

CAPTAINS, JUVENTUS' DINO ZOFF AND DENNIS MORTIMER SHAKE HANDS BEFORE THE EUROPEAN CUP QUARTER-FINAL FIRST LEG AT VILLA PARK

EUROPE

Aston Villa are one of only five English clubs to have won the European Cup (now called the UEFA Champions League). Some will say that the old European Cup format was harder to win because it only involved the champions of Europe's elite footballing nations.

There have been some very special European nights at Villa Park in the past, and they are nights to remember for sure, but none more so than those during the 1982 European Cup run.

Villa have actually won three European trophies and have competed in four different European competitions in their history.

TONY MORLEY AND ALLAN EVANS CELEBRATE AFTER WINNING THE EUROPEAN CUP FINAL AGAINST BAYERN MUNICH IN 1982

SEASONS IN EUROPE:	
1975/1976:	UEFA Cup First Round
1977/1978:	UEFA Cup quarter-final
1982:	European Cup Winners
1982/1983:	European Super Cup Winners
1983:	European Cup quarter-final
1983/1984:	UEFA Cup Second Round
1990/1991:	UEFA Cup Second Round
1993/1994:	UEFA Cup Second Round
1994/1995:	UEFA Cup Second Round
1996/1997:	UEFA Cup First Round
1997/1998:	UEFA Cup quarter-finals
1998/1999:	UEFA Cup Second Round
2001:	Inter-Toto Cup Winners
2001/2002:	UEFA Cup First Round
2008/2009:	Europa League Round of 32
2009/2010:	Europa League Play-Off Round
2010/2011:	Europa League Play-Off Round

RESULTS IN EUROPE (ALL COMPETITIONS):			
P	W	D	L
89	40	21	28

EUROPEAN CUP

Although the European Cup had first been competed for in 1955/1956, it wasn't until Aston Villa won the First Division title in 1980/1981 that they qualified for Europe's flagship club competition.

The fact that they won it at the first time of asking emulated the achievement of Nottingham Forest in 1978/1979. Villa's very first European Cup tie was at home to FC Valur and goals from Tony Morley, Terry Donovan (2) and Peter Withe (2) ensured the perfect start to their campaign. The return leg in Iceland saw Gary Shaw net twice to send Villa through to a second-round meeting with Dynamo Berlin. Morley was again on target, scoring a brace, as Villa won the away leg 2-1 so it didn't matter so much that the Germans won 1-0 at Villa Park because they went through on the away goals rule.

It would prove to be the last goal that Villa conceded en route to the final as goalkeeper Jimmy Rimmer was in superb form. Dynamo Kiev were dispatched 2-0 on aggregate while a solitary Morley goal in the first leg of the semi-final was enough to see off Anderlecht. That set up a clash with German champions, Bayern Munich in Rotterdam. Even the loss of Rimmer (replaced by youngster Nigel Spink making only his second appearance for the club)

after nine minutes could not give the Germans the advantage and Peter Withe scored the only goal of the night to send the Villa Park faithful wild and made history for Aston Villa FC.

Villa began their defence of the European Cup with a home tie against Besiktas. Goals from Withe, Morley and Mortimer gave the home side a 3-1 lead after the first-leg and ensured that the second leg in Turkey was merely a formality (this was drawn 0-0 to set up a clash with Dynamo Bucharest). The Romanians were no obstacle for a Villa side in full flow and a brace from Shaw in Bucharest laid the perfect foundation for an entertaining return tie at Villa Park. Gary Shaw was again on target in the second-leg, this time netting a hat-trick, and Mark Walters rounded up the scoring in a 4-2 victory. Juventus were Villa's opponents in the quarter-final, but the Italians proved too strong and emerged 5-2 victors over the two-legged tie.

The closest Villa have come to qualifying since was when they finished as runners-up to Manchester United in 1992/1993, but even though this was the inaugural season of the UEFA Champions League, and it was before more than one club was allowed to compete from each country.

THE VILLA TEAM CELEBRATE WITH THE UEFA SUPER CUP (BACK, L-R) GARY WILLIAMS, COLIN GIBSON, PETER WITHE, NIGEL SPINK, GARY SHAW; (FRONT ROW, L-R) ANDY BLAIR, DES BREMNER, MARK WALTERS, KEN McNAUGHT, GORDON COWANS, TONY MORLEY

EUROPEAN SUPER CUP

The European Super Cup was first competed for in 1973 and it pitted Europe's top two sides against each other. Traditionally played as the curtain raiser for the new season, the Cup was contested by the European Cup (now called the UEFA Champions League) and the European Cup Winners' Cup holders.

Since the abolition of the Cup Winners' Cup following the 1998/1999 final (ironically played at Villa Park), the match has featured the UEFA Cup winners (now called the Europa League).

As European Cup holders in 1982, Villa were paired with the European Cup Winners' Cup holders, Barcelona for the two-legged tie in January 1983. The first leg in Spain saw a solitary goal from Marcos Alonso Peña in the 52nd minute give the home side a slender advantage, but no-one would have been prepared for the way villa blew their opponents out of the water in the return match. Gary Shaw scored after 80 minutes to send the tie into extra-time and goals from Gordon Cowans and Ken McNaught sealed the victory.

FA CUP

The FA Cup is the longest running competition in world football, having first been contested in the 1871/1872 season. Aston Villa lie joint fifth (with Liverpool) in the table of English clubs that have won the most FA Cups. They have appeared in 11 finals, winning seven and being runners-up on four occasions.

Aston Villa first entered the FA Cup in the 1879/1880 season but had to wait until the second round to kick their first ball in the competition. They were handed a bye in the first round but faced Stafford Road for a place in the third round. A 1-1 draw at Perry Barr led to a replay which Villa won 3-1. Their opponents in the next round were Oxford University but the history books do not reveal why Villa failed to turn out for this fixture and the scholars were awarded the game.

it didn't take long, however, for Villa to get their hands on the trophy ...and when they did it ensured their place in the soon to be formed Football League. Villa registered their record Cup victory in the first round of the 1886/1887 competition en route to their first ever FA Cup final ...another West Midlands derby, this time against West Bromwich Albion.

Goals from Dennis Hodgetts and Archie Hunter secured the trophy that saw the streets of Birmingham packed with fans celebrating their famous victory.

The Villans imposed their dominance on the competition, winning the trophy another four times, 1-0 against West Brom in 1895; 3-2 against Everton in 1897 (completing the Double by claiming the First Division title); 2-0 against Newcastle United in 1905; and 1-0 against Sunderland in 1913 - before the First World War broke out. They also won the first competition following the end of hostilities with a 1-0 victory over Huddersfield town in 1920. The Villa Park faithful then had to endure another 37 years before their team lifted the trophy with a 2-1 victory preventing Manchester United from completing their own Double in the 1956/1957 season.

As previously mentioned, Villa have fallen at the final hurdle on four occasions. The first of these was in 1892 when West Brom gained their revenge with a 3-0 victory at the oval while Newcastle United also exacted retribution with a 2-0 triumph in 1924. Villa played Chelsea in the last FA Cup final played at the old Wembley and that ended in a 1-0 defeat. Villa's most recent appearance in the final was in 2015 when Arsenal trounced Villa 4-0.

THE CELEBRATIONS BEGIN AFTER THE FA CUP SEMI-FINAL PENALTY SHOOTOUT WIN OVER BOLTON, APRIL 2000

FAMOUS FANS

So why do so many famous people support Aston Villa FC? When you're talking of heavyweights, Aston Villa would knock you out with their list of famous fans. There is royalty, film icons, radio and TV presenters, MPs and sports stars among their many celebrity supporters.

As the largest club in the biggest UK city outside of London, it's understandable that Aston Villa have so many notable followers. But in terms of who takes the title of the most famous, it's hard to argue with Prince William. The future King of England was born less than a month after Villa's famous European Cup win in 1982 and seems to genuinely seems to love the club. He looked mightily upset when handing runners-up medals to his team in the 2015 FA Cup final and has gone on record about how much he loves Aston Villa. He's president of the FA too, which is more of a credential than most of us have to prove we love the beautiful game. He has been a Villa supporter ever since he saw his first live game (Aston Villa v Bolton Wanderers). And he's a fan of the Villa fans too, "Villa supporters are dedicated - they are great because, although Villa don't always win, they stay loyal," he says. The Duke of Cambridge can be seen at Villa Park

IAN LAVENDER
OF DAD'S ARMY FAME

(or Wembley) cheering on his team from the stands from time-to-time, with his son, George, and with his friend, former Villa legend, John Carew.

For Hollywood actor, Tom Hanks, he said after watching an Aston Villa match in London, "I thought I like their colours and I like the name, so I'm gonna be an Aston Villa man from now on!".

For other people, it's just in their blood.

For the former Prime Minister, David Cameron, his allegiance with Villa dates back watching games together with his uncle, Sir William Dugdale, former Villa chairman (1975 - 1978).

HERE'S A LIST OF VILLA'S MOST FAMOUS FANS:

THE MOST FAMOUS:

HRH Prince William (The Duke of Cambridge)
David Cameron (ex-Prime Minister)

ACTORS:

Tom Hanks
Martin Shaw (The Professionals)
Mark Williams (The Fast Show)
Brendan Gleeson (Harry Potter)
David Bradley (Harry Potter)
Oliver Phelps (Harry Potter)
Ian Lavender (Dad's Army)
Kris Marshall (Death in Paradise)
David Moran (Mind Your Language)
Nessa (Ruth Jones) from Gavin & Stacey

Lenny Godber from Porridge (fictional character)

Adil Ray (AKA Citizen Khan)

Greg Davies (comedian)

Helen George (Call the Midwife)

Domhnall Gleeson (Harry Potter)

Pauline McLynn (Father Ted)

MUSICIANS:

Geezer Butler (Black Sabbath)

Brian Travers (UB40)

Nigel Kennedy (violinist)

John Lodge (The Moody Blues)

Justin Hayward (lead singer of the Moody Blues)

Steve Winwood (Spencer Davis Group + Traffic)

Phil Etheridge (The Twang)

Pete Way (bassist with rock band UFO)

Chris Storr (plays trumpet in the Jools Holland Band)

Scott Gorham (original Thin Lizzy guitarist)

Dave Wakeling (The Beat)

Martin Duffy (Primal Scream)

Roger Taylor (Duran Duran)

TV & RADIO PRESENTERS:

Dr Carl Chinn MBE (local historian, tv & radio presenter)

Jonny Gould (media radio/tv broadcaster and commentator)

Emma B (Radio1 presenter)

Vassos Alexander (Radio 5 Live announcer)

Phil Williams (Radio 5 live announcer)

Matthew Bannister (Radio 5 Live)

Emma Willis (was Griffiths) (MTV presenter and model)

Pete Colley (Sky Sports reporter)

Floella Benjamin (80's TV Presenter)

Phil Upton (BBC Radio Coventry & Warwickshire)

Rupert Bell (talkSPORT Racing broadcaster)

SPORTS:

Dean Smith (former Villa manager)

Jack Grealish (former Villa captain)

Ian Taylor (Villa legend)

Ian Bell (Warwickshire and England cricketer)

Chris Woakes (Warwickshire and England cricketer)

Marc Albrighton (Leicester City player)

Dan Greaves (gold medal winning Paralympian)

Lee Sharpe (ex-Manchester Utd player)

Stan Collymore (ex-player, pundit)

Jane Sixsmith (England Olympic hockey player)

Tom Parsons (high jumper)

Craig Kieswetter (cricketer)

Dan Bailey (kicker for the Dallas Cowboys)

Katharine Merry (Olympic 400m bronze medallist)

MIX:

Mo Younis (Pride of Britain winner, ambassador for Acorns)

Gary Delaney (comedian)

Benjamin Zephaniah (poet)

Mervyn King (former Governor of Bank of England)

Jacqui Smith (former MP for Redditch and former Home Secretary)

Bill Morris (Trade Union leader)

Lord John Taylor (Baron Taylor of Warwick)

Sir Digby Jones (ex-head of the CBI)

Lee Child (Credited with being the author of Jack Reacher books)

Andrew Child (now the author of Jack Reacher book

KATHARINE MERRY CELEBRATES WINNING BRONZE IN THE 400M FINAL AT THE OLYMPIC GAMES, SYDNEY 2000

ABOVE:
ENGLAND CRICKETER IAN BELL

FORD

Welsh international, Trevor Ford played for his hometown club, Swansea City, including scoring a record 41 times in the 1945/1946 season, before moving to Aston Villa in 1947 for a fee of around £9,500 plus a player.

He was an old-school centre-forward, hard and uncompromising and always wanted to score goals like any good striker. He was renowned for shoulder-charging goalkeepers, an offence that would almost certainly be worthy of a sending off in modern-day football. Wales legend John Charles said that Ford was his idol, which was testament to the great player he was.

After his international debut in 1946, Ford went on to score a record-breaking 23 goals in 38 games for Wales, the most memorable being a back-heeled flick against England at Wembley in 1952. Ford was overlooked by Wales for the 1958 World Cup.

At Villa, he was a goal-machine, scoring a goal every other game on average. In his first season, he scored nine in the nine games he played in. When he left Villa for Sunderland in 1950, he became the most expensive forward in Britain at the age of 27, as the Roker Park outfit paid Villa £30,000 for him. Ford was outspoken for the reasons why he left

Villa, stating dissatisfaction with the lack of achievement at the club. Ironically, he failed to gain any major medals at Sunderland, even though Sunderland were known as 'The Bank of England club'.

He later had successful spells with Cardiff City (where he played with Gerry Hitchens before he himself came to Villa in 1957) and PSV Eindhoven, and he finished his league career with Newport County in 1960.

Like a few footballers in those days, Ford was a keen cricketer and played for Glamorgan a couple of times, including that famous game at Swansea when Sir Garfield Sobers hit six, sixes in one over.

He died in 2003 in Swansea at the age of 79.

ACTIVE SEASONS:	1946/1947 to 1950/1951
APPEARANCES:	128
GOALS:	61

GAS LAMP

On 21st November 1874, as legend tells us, four members of the Wesleyan Chapel male adult bible class met under a gas lamp in Heathfield Road, Perry Barr, Birmingham to form a football club called Aston Villa. The four founding fathers of the club are believed to be: Jack Hughes, William H Price, George Matthews and William H Scattergood.

Aston Villa FC were asked by a fan to make a place for a new lamp to be placed outside the entrance to the Holte Suite hospitality room outside the Villa Park stadium to pay homage to the founder members of the club.

The lamp was unveiled to the public before a Premier League game on 24th November 2014, some 140 years, almost to the day, after the club was officially formed. The lamp, named 'The Founding Lamp' and the idea was to get parents to explain to their kids the heritage and meaning behind it.

At the unveiling were descendants of Jack Hughes and William Scattergood.

AN ECSTATIC STEVEN GERRARD CELEBRATES THE
FIRST GOAL OF HIS REIGN AS VILLA BOSS AGAINST
BRIGHTON & HOVE ALBION, NOVEMBER 2021

RIGHT:
VILLA 2 BRIGHTON 0 AND GERRARD'S
FIRST THREE POINTS ARE IN THE BAG

GERRARD

Steven Gerrard was appointed Villa manager on 11th November 2021, replacing Dean Smith after three years and one month in charge at his boyhood club.

Gerrard was the standout candidate and brings with him his highly-rated back-room staff, including Gary McAllister, who was Gérard Houllier's assistant at Villa and replaced the Frenchman for two games at the end of the 2010/ 2011 season, winning both of them.

The 41-year-old brings a wealth of experience to Villa Park, being a one-club player at Liverpool, making 710 appearances winning nine trophies including three European titles, as well as 114 England caps. He is a leader, something that every team needs and for Villa, it means they have someone who has been there and done it in his time as a player.

After retiring from playing, Gerrard became Liverpool's Under-18 coach during the 2017/2018 season, before landing the Rangers Head Coach job in May 2018. During his three-and-a-half-year reign at Ibrox, he guided Rangers to their first win over Celtic since 2012, ending the league campaign nine points behind their city rivals, and they also finished second in the 2019/2020 season.

The following season saw Gerrard win his first piece of silverware as a manager, Rangers going unbeaten as they lifted the Scottish title for the 55th time, finishing an incredible 25 points clear of Celtic and also matched Celtic's 107-year-old clean-sheet record and won back-to-back Old Firm derbies.

It was Villa's CEO, Christian Purslow who was the key to appointing Gerrard at the helm, with the two forming a close bond during his days as Liverpool Managing Director. Villa moved quickly to make the appointment and it brings a fresh outlook and new ambition to Villa Park.

Purslow said after confirming the appointment of Gerrard, "Since moving into coaching after his illustrious playing career, Steven began by managing and developing top young players in the Liverpool FC Academy, which is experience we value highly at Aston Villa.

He then took the brave decision to test himself in the intense and high-pressured environment of the Scottish Old Firm. His subsequent achievement in winning the Premiership title with Glasgow Rangers really caught our eye as did his experience in Europe. It has been very clear in our discussions with him that Steven's coaching ambitions, philosophy and values entirely match those of Aston Villa."

For Gerrard, this is a huge leap from the SPL to the EPL, but it is also a huge leap in faith shown by Villa. In a statement following his appointment, Gerrard said, "Aston Villa is a club with a rich history and tradition in English football and I am immensely proud to become its new head coach. In my conversations with [co-owners] Nassef [Sawiris], Wes [Edens] and the rest of the board, it was apparent how ambitious their plans are for the club and I am looking forward to helping them achieve their aims."

Starting with a 2-0 home win against Brighton, exciting times are ahead for the Villa faithful.

GRAY

Born in Glasgow on 30 November 1955, Andy Gray began his football career as a striker for Dundee United where he made 62 appearances for the club and scored 46 goals before moving to Aston Villa in 1975.

It was his 25 league goals during the 1976/1977 campaign that earned him the PFA Young Player of the Year award as well as the PFA Players' Player of the Year, when he formed a lethal partnership, alongside Brian Little and John Deehan. Gray also shared the Golden Boot with Arsenal's Malcolm MacDonald. He became the first player to win both awards, a record that was only equalled in 2007 by Cristiano Ronaldo.

Gray was regularly capped for Scotland and played a total of 20 international matches between 1975 and 1985 and found the back of the net on seven occasions in his 10 years as an international.

Following his growing reputation at Villa, Gray moved to Wolves in 1979 for a then record fee of £1.4m where he spent the next four years making 133 appearances and scoring 38 goals. In 1983, he headed for Everton where he netted the ball 14 times in 49 appearances over two years. Gray had been a member of Everton's winning FA Cup side

in 1984 and won the First Division and a European Cup Winners' Cup medal in 1985 before returning to briefly Villa in 1985.

Once back at Villa, Gray's goalscoring ability continued but after just a year he went to Notts County on loan before permanently transferring to West Bromwich Albion in 1987, where spent a year with the club before moving back north to join Rangers (the team he supports) between 1988 and 1989. His final club was Cheltenham Town (1989 - 1990).

When he retired Gray returned to Villa for a third time as Ron Atkinson's assistant for a short time but found his niche as a football commentator and became a top-class football pundit on Sky Sports but was sacked from his high-profile position following some off-air sexist remarks.

He subsequently joined talkSPORT radio with co-presenter Richard Keys who was also sacked from Sky following the same alleged incident. Gray and Keys both now work for beIN Sports in Doha, Qatar.

ACTIVE SEASONS:	1975/1976 to 1986/1987
APPEARANCES:	210
GOALS:	78

GRAYDON

Ray Graydon was signed by Villa manager Vic Crowe in the summer of 1971 from his native Bristol Rovers and was virtually an ever-present in the team that won the Third Division title in his first season. Initially his signing caused a bit of a stir amongst Villa fans because the popular Brian Godfrey was part of the deal, and he went in the other direction.

Graydon became a very popular player after that and amassed well over 200 appearances over six seasons, with his highlight being the scorer from the rebound of his own penalty at the 1975 League Cup final against Norwich City at Wembley.

Graydon was a fast and busy player who seemed to be in the right place score some important goals for Villa. He was a player who was vital to Villa in their transition from the Third Division to the top league, Graydon was revitalized by Ron Saunders and seemed to find that process seamless - he was just as dangerous in whichever division he played in.

After a season interrupted by injury, Graydon earned his second League Cup medal 1977 before joining local rivals, Coventry City that summer for around £50,000. After a season with the Sky Blues, he played in the North American Soccer League for a summer before joining Oxford United before retiring as a player in 1981.

After he had hung up his boots, Graydon coached at Southampton, Oxford United, Watford, QPR and Port Vale before becoming manager at Walsall in May 1998. He led the club to promotion from the Second Division in the following season and repeated the feat via the play-offs in 2001. He was sacked by Walsall in 2002 and appointed Bristol Rovers manager later that year, but only lasted two years. He later briefly served as Leicester City's first-team coach.

RAY GRAYDON SCORES FROM THE REBOUND OF HIS OWN PENALTY KICK DURING THE 1975 LEAGUE CUP FINAL WIN OVER NORWICH CITY

ACTIVE SEASONS:	1971/1972 to 1976/1977
APPEARANCES:	232
GOALS:	81

'GOD'

Paul McGrath is fondly known to Villa fans a 'God' but life didn't throw any favours to the big Irishman when he was born on 4th December 1959. His Irish mother, terrified that her father would find out she was expecting a baby as the result of a relationship with a man from Nigeria, travelled to London to have her baby in secret.

The young McGrath, or Nwobilo, as was his name at the time, was brought up in a number of children's homes in Dublin. However, that didn't stop him from becoming one of Ireland's first celebrities of mixed race in later life.

The successful international began his career in defence with St Patrick's Athletic in Dublin before signing for Manchester United in April 1982 for £30,000. He was 22 when he joined Ron Atkinson at Old Trafford where he contributed to nearly 200 first team games with his reliable and solid state of play. He gained an FA Cup winner's medal in 1985 and scored 16 goals during his time with Manchester United.

After seven years with the Reds, he was signed by Villa manager, Graham Taylor for £450,000 in August 1989 where he was to become widely regarded as one of the greatest players to ever play for the club. The centre-back with dodgy knees who was allowed a less strenuous training regime proved he was reliable, controlled and good under pressure. His skills were instrumental to Villa when they beat McGrath's old team Manchester United in the League Cup final in 1994 - something he repeated two years later when Villa beat Leeds United in 1996.

In 1993 he was voted the PFA Players' Player of the Year.

McGrath moved to Derby County for a transfer fee of £100,000 in October 1996 and at the time he had already won 83 international caps for the republic of Ireland. One fabulous event occurred during the World Cup 1994 when Ireland were drawn to play reigning champions Italy.

Ireland were leading 1-0 when McGrath, who was marking Roberto Baggio, slid in front of his opponent, the ball was chipped into the air into the Irish player's face who then proceeded to chase the ball and deflate the Italians by denying them an equalising goal. McGrath had always been an integral part of the Irish team, particularly in the late 1980s and early 1990s under manager Jack Charlton.

Unfortunately, McGrath's likening of alcohol got in the way of his football at times, and there were occasions when he missed the occasional match or two. Additionally, he subsequently admitted he played under the influence on the odd occasion.

His 'dodgy knees' also hindered his career, and he had to undergo no fewer than eight operations during his career. Villa fans will say that Paul McGrath was a hell of a player, hence the nickname 'God', but a fit Paul McGrath would have been out of this world.

His autobiography, 'Back from the Brink was published in 2006 and duly won several awards.

ACTIVE SEASONS:	1989/1990 to 1996/1997
APPEARANCES:	323
GOALS:	9

A JUBILANT JACK AFTER VILLA HAD BEATEN DERBY COUNTY 2-1 IN THE PLAY-OFF FINAL AT WEMBLEY, 27 MAY 2019

LEFT:
YOUNG JACK DURING THE NEXTGEN SERIES QUARTER-FINAL, VILLA 1-0 OLYMPIAKOS, 20 MARCH 2013

GREALISH

Former Aston Villa captain, Jack Grealish has come a long way since his loan spell with Notts County in 2013 as a skinny 18-year-old to becoming the most expensive British footballer ever in the summer of 2021.

After making his full Villa debut in the 2014/2015 season, Jack came to life in the FA Cup semi-final against Liverpool in April 2015 and helped his side progress to the final. However, Villa lost that final badly to Arsenal and were relegated from the Premier League in the following season.

Playing under the radar in the Championship for three seasons, Jack found his talents were mainly hidden from wider world; however, the Villa faithful all knew he was a diamond in the making. It's no coincidence that Jack's favourite player when he was very young was Paul Merson, a former Villa playmaker and a footballer who oozed class himself.

Coming back from a long-term injury and becoming Villa captain in March 2019 seemed to be the making of him as Jack led Villa to a record 10 straight wins and led the club back into the big-time by helping his side win the EFL Championship Play-Off Final at Wembley.

Suddenly, 'Super Jack' attracted the attention of football fans right across the country (and the world) and he became the most talked about footballer in Europe; he became the most sought-after player on the planet, with all the top clubs looking at his next move.

England beckoned and eventually he got his chance, making his full international debut in September 2020.

Jack Grealish belongs in the Premier League, and it was no fluke that he led his Villa side to victory in May 2019, and subsequently, managed to cling on to their Premier League status on the final day of their first season.

In Villa's second season back in the Premier League, Jack (and Villa) got off to a flyer and everyone was talking about Europe, but a freak shin injury in training before an important game against Leicester City in February 2021 kept Jack out for three months and Villa's season started to crumble slightly, but when Jack returned for the last few games of the season, they finished on a high. Jack's injury threatened to ruin his pursuit of a Euro 2020 selection, but he returned to the fold just in time and made the final 23.

He got his chance in the Euros and made a major impact, with several cameo roles and a couple starring roles as England progressed to the final of Euro 2020 (which was played in the summer of 2021).

On 5th August 2021, Grealish, aged 25, signed for Manchester City for a British transfer record fee of £100m, leaving Villa fans disappointed that he didn't continue his Villa love affair. However, for Villa, they used some of that hefty transfer fee to secure the signings of Emi Buendia, Leon Bailey and Danny Ings.

ACTIVE SEASONS:	2014/2015 to 2020/2021
APPEARANCES:	213
GOALS:	32

HAMPTON

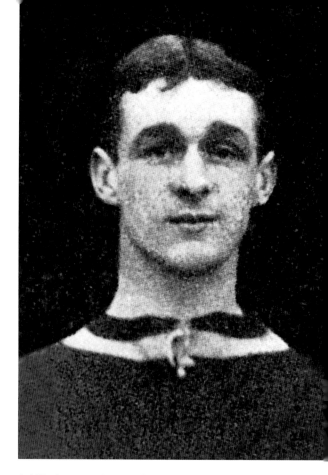

Joseph 'Harry' Hampton had the nicknames of "Happy" or "the Wellington Whirlwind", the latter named after the Shropshire town he was born in. The centre-forward played for Villa between the years of 1904 and 1920 and was a prolific striker who netted 242 times in his 372 appearances in all competitions.

In fact, he is Villa's record league goal-scorer with 215 goals in 338 games. 'Harry' once scored five in one match against Sheffield Wednesday in 1912.

He moved to Villa in April 1904 from Wellington Town on a free transfer and was renowned for being one of the most prolific strikers in the lead up to First World War. He was strong, forceful and dedicated and his determination and endurance meant that he was feared by goalkeepers and defenders alike. He was an exceptional player who was capped for England on four occasions for whom he found the back of the net twice.

At Villa, he won a League Championship medal in 1910 to go with the FA Cup winner's medal he received in 1905 (he won the FA Cup again eight years later) when he scored both goals in the final against Newcastle United. He fought in the First World War and regained his fitness quickly after a gas attack suffered during action. He was back playing football following military service where he continued to hammer home the ball for Birmingham City. After retiring from football, Hampton became a coach and died on 15 March 1963.

ACTIVE SEASONS:	1904/1905 to 1919/1920
APPEARANCES:	372
GOALS:	242

HENDRIE

Midfielder Lee Hendrie was the son of former Birmingham City player, Paul Hendrie and came through the Aston Villa youth system.

Villa fan, Lee, made his first-team debut for Villa on 23 December 1995 aged 18 against Queens Park Rangers when he came on as a substitute in a 1-0 defeat but was dismissed for two bookable offences.

However, his skills on the field earned him the Young Player of the Season award for 1997/1998 and his excellent touch gave Hendrie a chance to shine in the England Under-21s and he won a full cap when he came on as a substitute against the Czech Republic in 1999.

Lee was a controversial, precocious but sometimes remarkable on and off the pitch. In November 2005, in a head-butting incident on the pitch against Manchester City, Hendrie was reluctant to leave the field following the red card. He was warned about his violent behaviour and given a three-match ban by the FA Disciplinary Commission. David O'Leary had succeeded Graham Taylor by that time, and he virtually dropped Hendrie from the starting line-up.

Under Martin O'Neill, Hendrie continued to impress during the 2006/2007 campaign but was loaned to Stoke City in January 2007 before a permanent move to Sheffield United the following January. After only 12 league appearances for the Blades, Hendrie found himself out on loan with Leicester City but was unable to prevent them from being relegated to League One.

LEE HENDRIE IN ACTION, 1999/2000, AND LEFT, DURING THE 2001/02 CAMPAIGN

Hendrie's personal life has sometimes proved to be just as dramatic as his football career. In 2000, Hendrie stated that he would become tee-total during the football season following his three-month ban in international games for breaking the team curfew in the England Under-21s. However, in 2003, he was banned from driving for 12 months when he was stopped by police on the M40 for being one and a half times over the drink-drive limit.

He married his childhood sweetheart in 2004 but the marriage was over in hours after it was revealed that he had been seeing another woman. The honeymoon was subsequently cancelled, and Hendrie promptly moved in with his new partner.

His off-field activities have had a harmful influence on his career and his is a tragic story of unfulfilled potential and since leaving the Villa he played for myriad clubs without ever achieving a fraction of what he promised.

Hendrie retired from playing on 2014 at the age of 37 to start a football-based activities and events business for children called 'Footie Bugs'.

ACTIVE SEASONS:	**1996/1997 to 2006/2007**
APPEARANCES:	**308**
GOALS:	**32**

HITCHENS

Gerald Archibald Hitchens was born on 8 October 1934 in Rawnsley, Staffordshire and died in 1983 from a heart attack while playing in a charity match in North Wales. Despite his young age, perhaps it was a fitting end for the former miner who began his professional career with Kidderminster Harriers in 1953. Gerry then moved to Cardiff City two years later for a transfer fee of £1,500 after scoring a bucketful of goals for the Harriers.

He scored a dramatic goal on his league debut for Cardiff and the victory against Wolves that day helped keep his side in the First Division. At Cardiff, Hitchens built up an exceptional partnership with former-Villa legend, Trevor Ford and was the top goal-scorer in two successive campaigns finishing with a total of 40 times in his 95 appearances for the club. In 1957, his value had significantly increased, and he joined Aston Villa for £22,500.

GERRY BEFORE VILLA'S GAME AT CHELSEA 13 SEPTEMBER 1958

During his four seasons at Villa the fearless striker continued his impressive run of scoring goals. For three of the campaigns, Hitchens was Villa's leading striker between 1958 and 1961. In total, his 160 appearances for the club saw him find the back of the net no less than 96 times. In November 1959, he scored five of Villa's 11 goals against Charlton in an 11 - 1 victory, while his exceptional style of play saw him instrumental in Villa's campaign and their winning formula saw them become the top team in the Second Division.

The following year, Villa reached the League Cup final with the help of their heroic striker, although he didn't play in the final. He became a regular England Under-23 player before claiming his first full cap for the international side in 1961 at Wembley against Mexico where he scored just two minutes into the game.

It set the team up for an 8-0 victory over their opponents. It was the first of seven full caps for Hitchens who once again proved his talents two weeks after the victory of Wembley in a match in Rome where England beat their hosts 3=2, with two of the goals scored by Hitchens.

His prowess on the field brought him to the attention of Internazionale who signed Hitchens for £85,000 and he joined the likes of Joe Baker, Jimmy Greaves and Denis Law who were also playing in Italy at the time. It was the start of an eight-year career and love-affair with Italy.

However, it come at a cost as new England manager Alf Ramsey overlooked the confident striker in favour of home-based players, refusing to pick anyone who played abroad. His best season in Italy was his first, when he scored 18 goals in 37 league and cup appearances. Hitchens remained in Italy and subsequently played for Torino, Atalanta and Cagliari before returning to the UK to finish off his career in non-league football, then retiring to North Wales.

ACTIVE SEASONS:	1957/1958 to 1960/1961
APPEARANCES:	160
GOALS:	96

HOLTE END

Although Villa Park has been the home of Aston Villa since 1897, it wasn't until February 1940 that work was completed on building up the banking on what was now called the Holte End, which took its name from the Holte family and in particular, Sir Thomas Holte who built Aston Hall in the years between 1618 and 1631.

In the early years of the Aston Lower Grounds, the old name for what we now call Villa Park, the end was called the City End, the Church End before being named the Holte End.

In the 1940s, the Holte End stand was the largest in English football. It was originally open, with no roof, and was only partially covered in 1962 at a cost of around £40,000. It survived and remained untouched until the 1978/1979 season when health and safety was becoming the key issue in football ground thinking.

The Ibrox disaster led to the Safety of Sports Grounds Act of 1975 reduced the capacity of the Holte End and as a result new crush barriers were installed and the whole of the stand had to be re-terraced, whilst perimeter fences had been installed as well. When this work was finished the Holte End was capable of holding 22,600, the largest terrace capacity in England at that time but much lower previously years. A dividing fence was also installed to separate visiting supporters when the ground was used as a neutral venue, say for FA Cup semi-finals. However, this measure more than any other ruined the atmosphere of the Holte End.

The Hillsborough disaster in April 1989 had a significant effect on Villa Park and the Holte End. The immediate effect was the removal of the perimeter fencing and this reduced the capacity of the stand to 19,900. That decision didn't go down well with the fans, but it had to be done, given that health and safety rules were becoming paramount to the running of football clubs.

More changes came with the findings of the Taylor Report approved all-seater stadium in England by the 1994/1995 Premier League season. The Holte End roof was extended to cover the whole of the terrace, but it wasn't popular with the fans and didn't befit such an iconic stand.

Two supporting pillars were put in place that obscured the view for many fans. Then on 7th May 1994, the very last game was played in front of 45,347 fans (including the 19,900 standing fans in the Holte End terrace) as Villa beat Liverpool 2-1, with all three goals scored in front of the Holte. Following that game, the entire terrace was demolished and rebuilt in a Victorian-style red-brick design with a large two-tiered structure and a large mosaic denoting the club's name and badge.

The new structure was completed within a year and opened during the 1994/1995 season, with 13,500 seats and no pitch-side hospitality boxes.

HOUGHTON

ERIC HOUGHTON IN ACTION VS BRENTFORD, SEPTEMBER 1935

Eric Houghton signed for Aston Villa in August 1927 but didn't make his debut until over two years later, during the 1929/1930 season, when he scored **14 goals in 23 games in league and cup**. The following season, Houghton exploded onto the scene with **30 league goals in 41 appearances** during a season in which Villa scored an incredible 128 league goals, a First Division record and helped Villa to a runners-up place in the league.

That outstanding scoring record continued throughout his Villa career, with a goals-to-games ratio nearing one goal every other game. He spent nearly 19 years at Villa between the years of 1927 and 1946, although the Second World War interrupted his career. He was renowned for his dead-ball accuracy, scoring 58 penalties and 30 free-kicks during his career.

After leaving Villa in 1946, he played for Notts County for three seasons, where he finished his career at the age of 39. He then became Villa manager in 1953, taking over from George Martin, guiding them to a seventh FA Cup win in 1957 against the 'Busby Babes'. In the league, Villa continued to struggle and not even 'Mr Aston Villa' could help them, and he eventually was asked to resign in November 1958 when Joe Mercer took charge at Villa Park. Apparently, Houghton was a Villa fanatic, living and dreaming of Aston Villa every day.

Houghton was something of a phenomenon in that he was multi-skilled in sport; he also played first-class cricket for Warwickshire seven times in 1947, Lincolnshire in the minor counties and several club sides. He also won eight caps for the England football team.

Houghton returned to Villa Park for a third time in 1972 where he took a seat on the board and in 1983, he became senior vice-president of the club.

Houghton was among the first 12 former players and managers inaugurated into the Aston Villa Hall of Fame. He died aged 85 in May 1996 in Sutton Coldfield, West Midlands.

ACTIVE SEASONS:	1929/1930 to 1946/1947
APPEARANCES:	392
GOALS:	170

INTERNATIONALS ENGLAND

As of August 2021, there have been 76 players from Aston Villa who have represented England at international level, the first was Howard Vaughton in 1882 and the most recent being Ollie Watkins in 2021. To date, Villa have provided the second greatest number of players to represent England (with 76), just behind Tottenham Hotspur (with 78).

OLLIE WATKINS
CELEBRATES SCORING
ENGLAND'S FIFTH
VS SAN MARINO
WORLD CUP QUALIFIER
MARCH 2021

Here is a list of Villa's England internationals starting with the most recent. NB: caps gained only while playing for Villa:

1	Howard Vaughton (1882-1884)	5 caps, 6 goals
2	Arthur Brown (1882)	3 caps, 4 goals
3	Olly Whateley (1883)	2 caps, 2 goals
4	Albert Allen (1888)	1 cap, 3 goals
5	Dennis Hodgetts (1888-1894)	6 caps, 1 goal
6	Charlie Athersmith (1892-1900)	12 caps, 3 goals
7	Jack Devey (1892-1894)	2 caps, 1 goal
8	John Reynolds (1894-1897)	5 caps, 0 goals
9	Steve Smith (1895)	1 cap, 0 goals
10	Jimmy Crabtree (1896-1902)	11 caps, 0 goals
11	Howard Spencer (1897-1905)	6 caps, 0 goals
12	Fred Wheldon (1897-1898)	4 caps, 6 goals
13	Albert Wilkes (1901-1902)	5 caps, 1 goal
14	Billy George (1902)	3 caps, 0 goals
15	Billy Garraty (1903)	1 cap, 0 goals
16	Joe Bache (1903-1911)	7 caps, 4 goals
17	Billy Brawn (1904)	2 caps, 0 goals
18	Alec Leake (1904-1905)	5 caps, 0 goals
19	Albert Hall (1910)	1 cap, 0 goals

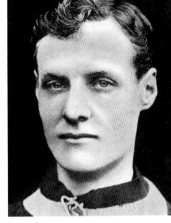

20	Harry Hampton (1913-1914)	4 caps, 4 goals
21	Charles Wallace (1913-1920)	3 caps, 0 goals
22	Sam Hardy (1913-1920)	7 caps, 0 goals
23	Frank Barson (1920)	1 cap, 0 goals
24	Andy Ducat (1920)	3 caps, 0 goals
25	Billy Walker (1920-1932)	18 caps, 9 goals
26	Billy Kirton (1921)	1 cap, 0 goals
27	Frank Moss (1921-1924)	5 caps, 0 goals
28	Tommy Smart (1921-1929)	5 caps, 0 goals
29	Richard York (1922-1926)	2 caps, 0 goals
30	George Blackburn (1924)	1 cap, 0 goals
31	Arthur Dorrell (1924-1925)	4 caps, 1 goal
32	Thomas Mort (1924-1926)	3 caps, 0 goals
33	Ben Olney (1928)	2 caps 0 goals
34	Eric Houghton (1930-1932)	7 caps, 5 goals
35	Joe Tate (1931-1932)	3 caps, 0 goals
36	'Pongo' Waring (1931-1932)	5 caps, 4 goals
37	George Brown (1932)	1 cap, 0 goals
38	Ronnie Starling (1937)	1 cap, 0 goals
39	Joe Beresford (1934)	1 cap, 0 goals
40	Thomas Gardner (1934-1935)	2 caps, 0 goals
41	Frank Broome (1938-1939)	7 caps, 3 goals
42	Eddie Lowe (1947)	3 caps, 0 goals
43	Tommy Thompson (1951)	1 cap, 0 goals
44	Gerry Hitchens (1961)	3 caps, 3 goals
45	Brian Little (1975)	1 cap, 0 goals
46	John Gidman (1977)	1 cap, 0 goals
47	Tony Morley (1981-1982)	6 caps, 0 goals
48	Peter Withe (1981-1984)	11 caps, 1 goal
49	Nigel Spink (1983)	1 cap, 0 goals
50	Gordon Cowans (1983-1990)	8 caps, 1 goal
51	Steve Hodge (1986)	11 caps, 0 goals

52	David Platt (1989-1991)	22 caps, 7 goals
53	Tony Daley (1991-1992)	7 caps, 0 goals
54	Earl Barrett (1993)	2 caps, 0 goals
55	Kevin Richardson (1994)	1 cap, 0 goals
56	Gareth Southgate (1995-2001)	42 caps, 1 goal
57	Ugo Ehiogu (1996)	1 cap, 1 goal
58	Stan Collymore (1997)	1 cap, 0 goals
59	Dion Dublin (1998)	1 cap, 0 goals
60	Lee Hendrie (1998)	1 cap, 0 goals
61	Paul Merson (1998)	1 cap, 0 goals
62	Gareth Barry (2000-2009)	29 caps, 2 goals
63	David James (2000-2001)	3 caps, 0 goals
64	Darius Vassell (2002-2004)	22 caps, 6 goals
65	Ashley Young (2007-2011)	5 caps, 2 goals
66	Scott Carson (2007)	2 caps, 0 goals
67	Gabriel Agbonlahor (2008-2009)	3 caps, 0 goals
68	Emile Heskey (2009-2010)	12 caps, 2 goals
69	James Milner (2009-2010)	12 caps, 0 goals
70	Stephen Warnock (2010)	1 cap, 0 goals
71	Darren Bent (2011)	6 caps, 3 goals
72	Stewart Downing (2011)	4 caps, 0 goals
73	Fabian Delph (2014-2015)	6 caps, 0 goals
74	Tyrone Mings (2019-2021)	16 caps, 1 goals
75	Jack Grealish (2020-2021)	12 caps, 0 goals
76	Ollie Watkins (2021)	5 caps, 1 goal

GARETH SOUTHGATE
1996/97

LEFT:
BILLY BRAWN,
CAPPED BY
ENGLAND 1904

INTERNATIONALS UK & IRELAND

Aston Villa have not only contributed to England international teams of the past and present, but they have also produced some incredible stars for the other home international teams. Here is the entire list as of August 2021.

SCOTLAND

Believe it or not, there have only been 15 Scotland internationals who have played for Villa. The list includes:

1	**Jimmy Cowan** (1896-1898)	3 caps, 0 goals
2	**Robert Templeton** (1902-1904)	4 caps, 1 goal
3	**Thomas Niblo** (1904)	1 cap, 0 goals
4	**James Gibson** (1927-1930)	4 caps, 1 goal
5	**Danny Blair** (1932)	1 cap, 0 goals
6	**Alex Massie** (1936-1937)	7 caps, 1 goal
7	**George Cummings** (1936-1939)	6 caps, 0 goals
8	**Andy Gray** (1975-1978)	6 caps, 2 goals
9	**Allan Evans** (1982)	4 caps, 0 goals
10	**Alan McInally** (1989)	2 caps, 1 goal
11	**Colin Calderwood** (1999)	4 caps, 0 goals
12	**Shaun Maloney** (2007-2008)	9 caps, 0 goals
13	**Barry Bannan** (2010-2013)	2 caps, 0 goals
14	**Alan Hutton** (2011-2016)	7 caps, 0 goals
15	**John McGinn** (2018-2021)	40 caps, 11 goals

WALES

1	**Walter Evans** (1891-1892)	2 caps
2	**Alfred E Watkins** (1900)	2 caps
3	**Arthur Green** (1901)	1 cap
4	**Walter M Watkins** (1904)	3 caps
5	**Ioan Price** (1907)	1 cap
6	**Robert Evans** (1907-1908)	3 caps
7	**David Astley** (1931-1936),	3 caps
8	**Cuthbert Phillips** (1936-1937)	9 caps
9	**Thomas Griffiths** (1936-1937)	4 caps
10	**Trevor Ford** (1947-1950)	13 caps
11	**Keith Jones** (1949)	1 cap
12	**Ivor Powell** (1949-1950)	4 caps
13	**Vic Crowe** (1958-1962)	16 caps
14	**Phil Woosnam** (1963)	2 caps
15	**Barry Hole** (1968-1969)	4 caps
16	**Trevor Hockey** (1973)	1 cap
17	**Leighton Phillips** (1974-1978)	27 caps
18	**Dean Saunders** (1992-1995)	14 caps
19	**Mark Delaney** (1999-2006)	36 caps
20	**Robert Edwards** (2003-2004)	4 caps
21	**James Collins** (2009-2011)	9 caps
22	**James Chester** (2016-2018)	14 caps
23	**Neil Taylor** (2017-2019)	6 caps

IRELAND (COMBINED)

1	**William Renneville** (1911)	1 cap
2	**Thomas Muldoon** (1927)	1 cap

NORTHERN IRELAND

1	**Con Martin** (1948-1950)	2 caps
2	**Danny Blanchflower** (1951-1954)	9 caps
3	**Norman Lockhart** (1953-1956)	14 caps
4	**Peter McParland** (1954-1961)	33 caps
5	**Derek Dougan** (1962)	3 caps
6	**Sammy Morgan** (1973-1975)	8 caps
7	**Chris Nicholl** (1974-1977)	12 caps
8	**Steve Davis** (2005-2007)	20 caps
9	**Aaron Hughes** (2005-2007)	11 caps

REPUBLIC OF IRELAND

1	**Con Martin** (1948-1956)	24 caps
2	**David Walsh** (1951-1953)	6 caps
3	**Pat Saward** (1957-1960)	13 caps
4	**Alfred Hale** (1962)	1 cap
5	**Terry Donovan** (1979-1981)	2 caps
6	**Eamonn Deacy** (1982)	4 caps
7	**Paul McGrath** (1989-1996)	51 caps
8	**Tony Cascarino** (1990-1991)	14 caps
9	**Steve Staunton** (1991-2002)	64 caps
10	**Ray Houghton** (1992-1994),	16 caps
11	**Andy Townsend** (1993-1997)	28 caps
12	**Gareth Farrelly** (1996)	3 caps
13	**Mark Kinsella** (2002-2004)	15 caps
14	**Stephen O'Halloran** (2007)	2 caps
15	**Richard Dunne** (2009-2012)	23 caps
16	**Shay Given** (2011-2015)	24 caps
17	**Ciaran Clark** (2011-2016)	24 caps
18	**Conor Hourihane** (2017-2021)	36 caps

SHAY GIVEN

LEFT:
JAMES COLLINS

JOACHIM

Julian Joachim (JJ) turned professional with Leicester City in September 1992 and spent four years with the Foxes, scoring 31 goals in 119 appearances before Brian Little signed him for Villa in February 1996 for £1.5m, having managed JJ at Filbert Street.

He was lightning quick and had the ability to confuse the opposition's defence, but at Villa he found himself facing competition from the likes of Dwight Yorke, Savo Milošević and Tommy Johnson. He did, however, score on his debut for Villa against Blackburn Rovers, but the constant competition did little to improve his first team chances. It gave rise to a slow start at Villa for Joachim. However, the 1997/1998 campaign proved more fruitful for the exceptional striker and a regular first team place inspired the fans and made him a firm favourite.

Like many other good players Joachim was faced with ups and downs and injuries that blighted his form, but overall, his time at Villa was spent scoring stunning goals and he was voted the club's Player of the Year in 1999. The arrival of Benito Carbone in 1999 did see Joachim on the bench on a number of occasions, but a window of opportunity opened for the striker when Dion Dublin found himself out of the game for just over three months of the season and provided Joachim with a place on an ever-skilful forward line for Villa. JJ was a talented youngster and played for England at Under-18, Under-19 and nine appearances at Under-21 level, although he didn't break into the full squad.

It all changed for the striker in July 2001 during the summer transfer window when Joachim was sent to local rivals Coventry City in a player-exchange with Mustapha Hadji which cost the club £2m. Three years later, in June 2004, Joachim found himself heading to Leeds United on a free transfer. The player's new club were at the time heavily in debt and in the process of trying to rebuild the team, if somewhat inexpensively. His season with Leeds was disappointing and he only managed two goals in his 27 appearances. He then found himself loaned to Walsall for the final two months of the campaign. He moved to Boston United for the 2005/2006 season where he joined the team in League Two and scored 17 goals in 46 appearances. Then, on 14 August 2006, Joachim joined Darlington for £100,000 - a record fee for his new club. In recent times, even at his advanced years, JJ has appeared for Nottinghamshire Senior League team, Aslockton & Orston in July 2018 and played 39 times. At the age of 43, JJ signed for Bourne Town.

ACTIVE SEASONS:	1995/1996 to 2000/2001
APPEARANCES:	172
GOALS:	45

KITS
CLUB COLOURS

Aston Villa are one of only a few sides in England who wear a kit comprising of claret and blue. The others include West Ham United, Burnley and Scunthorpe United. However, that has not always been the case; in the club's early days they wore kits that included blue/red, black, red, shades of green and blue/white and the minutes of a meeting in November 1886 confirmed that a chocolate/sky blue outfit was to be worn by the players, a kit they had worn during the 1886/1887 FA Cup winning campaign.

By the following year, in 1887, one year before the formation of the Football League, Villa had adopted their now famous claret and blue colours although there are several possible theories behind the reason for this decision. One suggested that the directors were unable to decide at a meeting in the local Barton's Arms public house and that they took their inspiration from the coloured tiles on the walls of the pub. Another, perhaps more plausible explanation is that it was suggested by the Scottish contingent prevalent at Villa at the time and combined the blue of Glasgow Rangers with the maroon of Hearts and that the crest should include the rampant lion of Scotland.

Since 1893, the body of the kit has been claret and the arms a sky-blue colour, and white shorts have been predominately worn, although there has been some tinkering in more recent times, when kit designers became more liberal. This occurred between the 1983/1984 and 1986/1987 seasons, and again between 1993 and 1995 and the 1999/2000 season, when the body and arms were claret and blue stripes of differing width. During the 2001/2002 season and again during the 2018/2019 season, Villa went against traditional again and the entire shirt was claret, with only snippets of blue on the sleeve and collar.

**CONOR HOURIHANE
IN THE ALMOST
ALL-CLARET SHIRT FROM
THE 2028/19 PLAY-OFF
WINNING CAMPAIGN**

KIT DESIGNS

In the early part of the twentieth century, the Villa kits featured drawstring lacing at the collar, but this design was modified in 1924, when the kits contained high crew-neck collars, and the lacing was discarded. In the mid-1950s, the high neckline design was discarded in favour of a 'V' neck design. That lasted until the 1963/1964 season, when a round-neck design was introduced. The 1970s saw the introduction of the collar and between 1974 and 1981 a collar and a 'V' neck was introduced, and this became an iconic shirt. This was then followed by the 'V' neck and no collar shirt as seen during the club's successful League Championship and European Cup triumphs. Since then, kits changed every two years until that is, when sponsorships took over in the late 1990s and the kit designs changed annually. Nowadays, there doesn't seem to be any consistency with regards the collar, one season it's a 'V' neck, the next a rounded collar, or even buttoned-up collars.

Strangely enough, the traditional drawstrings design returned for the 1992/1993 season and the introduction of the FA Premier League, the season Villa finished runners-up to Manchester United, but that only lasted one season and split the opinions of the fans.

AWAY KITS

Villa's away kits have changed in colour many times over the years, from sky blue during the late 1950s and early 1960s, to white, black, green, black and red stripes, dark blue and yellow. The most iconic away kit was the one worn during the 1957 FA Cup final. It was predominately sky blue with claret pinstripes. Another iconic away shirt was worn during the 1982 European Cup final. That kit was predominately white and also featured thin claret pinstripes.

SPONSORSHIPS

Radical changes appeared on the shirts during the 1970s, with shirt and sports manufacturers beginning to influence designs and during the early 1980s, sponsorships were to be seen on shirts; Villa's first shirt sponsor was Davenports (a local brewery) during the 1982/1983 season. Shirt sponsors change as quickly as shirt manufacturers these days and it's hard to keep up with who sponsors the shirts season in, season out.

Here is a list of club sponsors throughout the club's history:

1982/1983 (ONE SEASON):

Club shirt sponsors: Davenports
Shirt manufacturers: Le Coq Sportiff

1984/1985 (ONE SEASON):

Club shirt sponsors: Mita
Shirt manufacturers: Le Coq Sportiff

1985-1987 (TWO SEASONS):

Club shirt sponsors: Mita
Shirt manufacturers: Henson.

1987-1990 (THREE SEASONS):

Club shirt sponsors: Mita Copiers
Shirt manufacturers: Hummel

1990-1993 (THREE SEASONS):

Club shirt sponsors: Mita Copiers
Shirt manufacturers: Umbro

1993-1995 (TWO SEASONS):

Club shirt sponsors: Muller
Shirt manufacturers: Asics

1995-1998 (THREE SEASONS):

Club shirt sponsors: AST Computer
Shirt manufacturers: Reebok

1998-2000 (TWO SEASONS):

Club shirt sponsors: LDV Vans
Shirt manufacturers: Reebok

2000-2002 (TWO SEASONS):

Club shirt sponsors: NTL
Shirt manufacturers: Diadora

2002-2004 (TWO SEASONS):

Club shirt sponsors: Rover
Shirt manufacturers: Diadora

2004-2006 (TWO SEASONS):

Club shirt sponsors: DWS
Shirt manufacturers: Hummel

2006/2007 (ONE SEASON):

Club shirt sponsors: 32 Red.com
Shirt manufacturers: Hummel

2007/2008 (ONE SEASON):

Club shirt sponsors: 32 Red.com
Shirt manufacturers: Nike

2008-2010 (TWO SEASONS):

Club shirt sponsors: Acorns
Shirt manufacturers: Nike

2010/2011 (ONE SEASON):

Club shirt sponsors: FXPro
Shirt manufacturers: Nike

2011/2012 (ONE SEASON):

Club shirt sponsors: Genting Casinos
Shirt manufacturers: Nike

2012/2013 (ONE SEASON):

Club shirt sponsors: Genting Casinos
Shirt manufacturers: Macron

2013-2015 (TWO SEASONS):

Club shirt sponsors: Dafabet
Shirt manufacturers: Macron

2015/2016 (ONE SEASON):

Club shirt sponsors: QuickBooks
Shirt manufacturers: Macron

2016/2017 (ONE SEASON):

Club shirt sponsors: QuickBooks
Shirt manufacturers: Under Armour

2017/2018 (ONE SEASON):

Club shirt sponsors: Unibet
Shirt manufacturers: Under Armour

2018/2019 (ONE SEASON):

Club shirt sponsors: 32Red
Shirt manufacturers: Luke1977

2019/2020 (ONE SEASON):

Club shirt sponsors: W88
Shirt manufacturers: Kappa

2020-2022 (TWO SEASONS):

Club shirt sponsors: Cazoo
Shirt manufacturers: Kappa

DANNY INGS
2021/22

LAURSEN

Martin Laursen had won the Champions League (2003) and Serie A (2004) with AC Milan and had come with good pedigree when Villa paid a modest £3m for him in the summer of 2004. However, throughout the five seasons he spent at Villa Park, Danish international Laursen had been dogged by knee problems which restricted him to a dozen games in his debut season in 2004/2005 and just one in his second season.

By the end of his third season, he hadn't managed 30 appearances for Villa, but then we discovered just why Villa had paid Italian giants AC Milan £3m for him back in 2004.

The 2007 - 2008 campaign was an unqualified success for Laursen, who was not only an ever-present in the Premier League but also weighed in with nine goals. His commanding performances and scoring feats earned him the Supporters' Player of the Year award in that season - and it got even better. He was appointed club captain at the start of the 2008 - 2009 campaign, he was a colossus at the heart of the defence as Villa broke into the top four under Martin O'Neill and made progress in the UEFA Cup.

His scoring feats continued too, including the crucial early opening goal against Ajax in a UEFA Cup group game at Villa Park, while he was also named Danish Footballer of the Year. Laursen was capped 53 times by Denmark, which seems amazing, given he only appeared 91 times for Villa in five seasons.

Disaster hit Laursen at West Ham just before Christmas 2008 as he went down injured, and so it proved to the beginning of the end for his career. However, Laursen returned for the home game against West Bromwich Albion three weeks later, but it proved to be his last before his premature retirement in 2009.

Laursen will remain a Villa legend because he was a true professional and seemed to love wearing the claret & blue shirt of Aston Villa, having an excellent rapport with the fans during his short but fruitful career.

ACTIVE SEASONS:	2004/2005 to 2008/2009
APPEARANCES:	91
GOALS:	11

LEAGUE CHAMPIONSHIP

The formation of the Football League in **1888** owed much to the determination of William McGregor, a Scotsman who had seen his first football match at the age of eight and who became associated with Aston Villa soon after the club was formed in **1874**. He went on to serve the club as a director, vice-chairman and was chairman between **1894** and **1902**. It was McGregor who pushed for a professional league to be set up and Villa were one of the **12** founder members.

Aston Villa finished runners-up to Preston in the inaugural season but claimed their first title in 1893/1894. Villa dominated the 1890s in much the same way that Liverpool did in the 1970s and 1980s and Manchester United in the 1990s and early 21st century. Villa won back-to-back titles in 1895/1896 and 1896/1897 (the same year they triumphed in the FA Cup to claim the Double) and repeated this after finishing sixth the following season. Indeed, when they won their fifth championship in 1899/1900, they set a new record of 50 points from 34 games. They topped the Division One table again in 1909/1910 and also narrowly missed out a further five times before the advent of the First World War when they finished second.

Sadly, that was to prove their last league title for more than 70 years - although they were runners-up in 1930/1931 and 1932/1933 - and the unthinkable happened in 1936 when

they were relegated to the Division Two for the (then) first time in their history. They bounced back at the second attempt claiming the Division Two crown in 1937/1938 and remained in the top-flight until they suffered another relegation in 1959. This time their stay in the second tier only lasted one season but there followed a period of instability that saw the club return to the Division Two in 1967 and drop to the third tier in 1970.

Promotions in 1972 and 1975 saw Villa regain their top-flight status again, a position they have held ever since apart from one season in the second tier in 1987/1988. Villa's most recent of their seven top-flight titles came in 1980/1981 when manager Ron Saunders used just 14 players (seven of whom were ever-present) and the club were runners-up to Liverpool in 1989/1990.

CELEBRATIONS IN THE DRESSING ROOM AT HIGHBURY AFTER WINNING THE 1980/81 FOOTBALL LEAGUE CHAMPIONSHIP

LEAGUE CUP

Aston Villa rank third only to Liverpool and Manchester City when it comes to success in the Football League Cup, with nine final appearances resulting in five trophies. They have also been losing semi-finalists on four occasions since the competition's debut in 1960/1961.

The idea of a League Cup competition had been proposed as far back as 1892 yet it was only when the former League secretary Alan Hardaker pushed for its inception that it became a reality in the early 1960s. From its inception, the competition had no main title sponsor, but since 1981, the tournament has had many sponsors and been known as the Milk Cup (1981-1986), Littlewoods Cup (1986-1990), Rumbelows Cup (1990 - 1992), Coca-Cola Cup (1992-1998), Worthington Cup (1998-2003) Carling Cup (2003-2012), Capital One Cup (2012-2015) until its current guise of the Carabao Cup from 2017. There was only one year when there wasn't a sponsor and that was during the 2016/2017 season when it was known as the EFL Cup.

Many of the bigger clubs refused to enter the competition in its early years until the final was moved to Wembley in 1967 (prior to this it had been played over two legs at the participants' home grounds) and victory ensured entry into the following season's UEFA Cup. Aston Villa were one of the top-flight teams who did enter the inaugural competition and they emerged triumphant with a 3-0 extra-time victory over Rotherham United in the second leg after losing the first game by 2-0.

They were back in the final two years later and this time their opponents were local rivals Birmingham City, but Villa lost the first leg 3-1 and could only manage a 0-0 draw in the return match.

They almost made it three final appearances in five years but fell at the semi-final stage in 1965. Tony Hateley had grabbed seven goals in the earlier rounds - including four in the 7-1 fifth-round demolition of Bradford City - but despite scoring another three over the two-legged clash Chelsea progressed to the final with a 4-3 aggregate score.

Villa appeared in three finals in the 1970s, claiming the trophy twice (they lost 2-0 against Spurs in 1971 but beat Norwich City 1-0 in 1975 and Everton 3-2 in 1977) but the furthest they progressed in the 1980s was two semi-finals (1984 and 1986).

They did add their name to the trophy in 1994 and 1996 with victories over Manchester United (a 3-1 win against manager Ron Atkinson's former club) and Leeds United (3-0) but the closest they recently came to adding to their tally was in the 2010 final against Manchester United where James Milner scored an early penalty, but United replied with goals from Michael Owen and Wayne Rooney and a 2-1 defeat to Manchester City in 2020.

JOHN BURRIDGE AND CHRIS NICHOLL CELEBRATE WITH THE TROPHY AFTER THEIR 3-2 EXTRA-TIME VICTORY IN THE 1977 LEAGUE CUP FINAL SECOND REPLAY

LEFT:
COCA COLA CUP WINNERS 1994

Aston Villa's League Cup record	
1960/1961	Winners
1962/1963	Runners-up
1970/1971	Runners-up
1974/1975	Winners
1976/1977	Winners
1993/1994	Winners
1995/1996	Winners
2009/2010	Runners-up
2019/2020	Runners-up

LITTLE

It all began for Brian Little with Aston Villa when he signed for the then Third Division team on leaving school in 1970. Little progressed through the youth team and in his 302 appearances for the club he scored 82 times. Little found himself in two League Cup winning teams for Villa in 1975 and 1977 and won his only full cap for England in May 1975 against Wales at Wembley.

Despite his silky skills on the pitch, his career was cut short when he suffered a serious knee injury in 1979. He was a favourite with the fans and had a reputation for being a Villa Park legend, with the fans singing, "Brian Little walks on water...".

Despite his serious injury, his career was far from over and Little remained on the Villa payroll as a youth team coach. He then coached the first team at Wolves who were being relegated to the Fourth Division for the first time in 1986. The debts at the club were immense and when John Barnwell resigned as manager, Little took the reins on a temporary basis but was later replaced by Graham Turner.

Little then moved to Middlesbrough as first team coach, but the club was also in financial difficulties and narrowly missed bankruptcy. However, with help from Little and other members of the staff, including Bruce Rioch, the club slowly improved and saw themselves promoted on two successive occasions to play in the First Division for the 1988/1989 season. Little left for Darlington to become manager at the end of the season where his new team sat squarely at the bottom of the Football League in the Fourth Division, but by the end of the 1990/1991 season he saw his club win the Fourth Division Championship.

In June 1991, Leicester City appointed him manager as successor to Gordon Lee and he took the Second Division club to fourth place by the end of the season.

After a great deal of hard work and determination by both manager and players, Leicester gained a place in the Premier League during the 1993/1994 campaign on their third attempt via the play-off route.

Having increased his stock enormously, Little acrimoniously left the Foxes and took the job of manager at Aston Villa in November 1994 and led the team to the 1996 League Cup final and won the trophy, beating Leeds United 3-0. Four years later he was manager of Stoke City and then West Bromwich Albion in 1999. He moved to Hull City in 2000,

Tranmere rovers in 2003 and on to Wrexham in 2007. Unfortunately, the Red Dragons lost their league status with relegation from League Two at the end of 2007/2008 and Little parted company to go to Northern Conference side, Gainsborough Trinity, until he was sacked in 2011.

Brian Little is now an advisor to the Board of Aston Villa FC.

BRIAN NETS THE WINNING GOAL PAST EVERTON GOALKEEPER DAVID LAWSON IN THE 1977 LEAGUE CUP FINAL

ACTIVE SEASONS:	1971/1972 to 1979/1980
APPEARANCES:	302
GOALS:	82

LOGOS

From the time Villa became a founder member of the Football League in 1888, there wasn't an official club badge or logo on the shirts, even though the club's heritage has always been represented by a heraldic lion by the club's founders.

It wasn't until the 1956/1957 season that the rampant lion appeared on Villa shirts, although there was a Villa crest which included a lion and the word 'Prepared' from 1878. That first badge remained on the shirts until 1969, when the word 'Prepared' was dropped from the badge, replaced by 'AV' underneath the lion, which itself had been re-designed slightly.

VILLA CREST USED FROM 1956 ALONGSIDE PRESENT DAY CREST

In 1975 a brand-new round badge appeared on the club's shirts, again without the word 'Prepared', but this time the lion was surrounded by the words 'Aston Villa FC'. This round badge was a huge hit with the fans, and still is, with many fans longing for the return of it. In 1992, the badge was re-designed again, this time the lion appeared in yellow instead of claret and was cast within a shield design with claret and blue background. The word 'Prepared' reappeared within the shield, along with 'Aston Villa' at the top of the badge.

With the ownership moving from Sir Doug Ellis to Randy Lerner in 2006, the badge was redesigned yet again, this time in the 2007/2008 season, when the emergence of a white star within the shield signifying the club's single European Cup win. The words 'Aston Villa' were replaced by 'AVFC' and 'Prepared' remained within the re-shaped shield.

Like all football clubs, Aston Villa have evolved and so have their logos, with at least eight iterations of its badge in the club's history. The last iteration took place before the 2016/2017 season, when some subtle changes were made. From fan feedback before that season, the claws included a greater emphasis on the rampant lion, and the lion itself appeared smaller within the shield and the word 'Prepared' was removed again.

While the word 'Prepared' is part of the club's heritage, it soon became a contentious issue to remove the word from the club's logo in 2016, and in some circles, it still is. There have been calls from supporters and supporters' groups for the club to consider returning to the round badge, but this hasn't yet materialised, although the new owners (Edens and Sawiris) may still have their own ideas in due course.

LYNN

Stan Lynn was a solid, hard-tackling, old-fashioned full-back who had a thunderbolt shot on him.

He served Villa in a defensive role for more than a decade during the 1950s until 1961, when he was signed by near neighbours, Birmingham City, but by then he had lost much of his pace. His powerful shooting was always a big talking point among the fans, but he was more than a solid full-back. His 38 goals in 324 appearances for Villa gave him an average of more than one every 10 games - and he became the first full-back to score a top-light hat-trick, including two penalties, in a 5-2 victory over Sunderland in January 1958, and remains one of the highest-scoring full-backs in football history, with a total of 70 goals spanning more than 500 games.

Lynn was signed by Villa from Lancashire club, Accrington Stanley in March 1950 for a fee said to be around £10,000, and he was on target three times before the end of that season, with two of them coming when he operated as an emergency centre-forward. Throughout the course of the next 10 seasons, Lynn was Villa's regular right-back, but he suffered some injury problems that meant he was only an ever-present when Villa won the Second Division title in 1959/1960.

STAN LYNN BEFORE THE GAME AT ARSENAL, OCTOBER 1957

He helped the club to win two major trophies, FA Cup glory over Manchester United in 1957, and he played in the first leg of the first ever League Cup final against Rotherham in 1961. Ironically, he picked up another League Cup medal two years later, when Birmingham City beat Villa in the 1963 final.

After retirement, he continued to play for the Aston Villa Old Stars until 1985.

He died in 2002 in a Birmingham nursing home after suffering from Alzheimer's at the age of 73.

ACTIVE SEASONS:	1950/1951 to 1961/1962
APPEARANCES:	324
GOALS:	38

MELLBERG

Swedish defender Olof Mellberg made his name playing in his native Sweden for Degerfors and AIK Solna between 1996 and 1999. His skills and talents took him to Spanish club Racing Santander, where he spent two seasons and made 97 appearances until the end of the 2000/2001 season when the club were relegated.

Mellberg joined Aston Villa on 19 July 2001 for £5.6m, and he made his debut on the opening day of the new season against Tottenham Hotspur. Despite missing a number of games during that season due to injury, the tall Swede made a great impression at Villa Park and is now considered to be a 'legend' with the fans. He proved his worth during Villa's 2002/2003 campaign when he was a regular on the first team, had a strong campaign with during the successful 2003/2004 season and was equally impressive during the following season when he made 33 league appearances for the club.

However, he suffered an untimely knee injury in April 2005 but returned for the 2005/2006 season to continue his defence in Villa's back line. In January 2008, during a typically solid season, it was announced that Mellberg would be joining Juventus on a three-year contract in that summer. Mellberg, holder of more than 75 caps for Sweden (69 while playing for Villa) did not bring any funds into Martin O'Neill's kitty, however, as he left on a free transfer under the Bosman ruling.

Although Mellberg announced his intention of leaving Villa halfway through the season, he remained solid and consistent. At his last match for the club, an away trip to West Ham on 11th May 2008, he made a gesture to the 3,200 travelling fans that will never be forgotten - he bought every one of the away fans a replica shirt to remember him by, with the words 'Thanks 4 Your Support' on the back.

ACTIVE SEASONS:	2001/2002 to 2007/2008
APPEARANCES:	263
GOALS:	8

McPARLAND

Irishman, Peter McParland will always be known for his two goals for Villa that beat the Busby Babes in the 1957 FA Cup Final.

McParland was spotted by Villa from Irish side, Dundalk by former manager, George Martin in 1952, costing £3,500 to bring him to Birmingham. However, Martin didn't give the then teenager his debut, that was down to Eric Houghton, who coached McParland and made him a better player, honing his skills and goal-scoring ability in the way Houghton played before the War. Villa coach Jimmy Hogan had an equally positive effect on McParland, who later blossomed into a fine winger.

It wasn't until the 1956/1957 season that McParland began to shine, and it was his goals that helped Villa to FA Cup glory in that season. The significant memory that Villa fans will remember, apart from his two goals in that Wembley final, will be the collision of heads with Manchester Untied goalkeeper, Ray Wood, which effectively put Wood out of the game.

In 1958, McParland was picked by Northern Ireland at the World Cup finals in Sweden, and he demonstrated his goalscoring prowess again and had a remarkable impact on that competition, which saw the Irish get to the quarter-finals. In all, McParland was capped 34 times by his country and scored 10 goals.

After 10 seasons with Villa, scoring 121 goals, McParland was transferred to Wolves for £30,000 in 1962, but that career was short-lived. After retiring from playing, he later became the national coach of Cyprus and then became player-manager of Irish club, Glentoran.

Now 87 (at the time of writing), McParland lives on the south coast of England.

PETER McPARLAND AT CHELSEA DECEMBER 1954

ACTIVE SEASONS:	1952/1953 to 1961/1962
APPEARANCES:	341
GOALS:	121

MERSON

Despite personal difficulties, Paul Merson, had a prolific career as a forward, midfielder and less so, a manager. His skill and influence on the game was instrumental, while his popularity as a person and a player was always high.

He began his career with Arsenal when he joined the club as an apprentice in 1982 and, after a spell on loan to Brentford, he made his debut for the Gunners against Manchester City in 1986. He was an integral part of the Arsenal team during the late 1980s, but it was during the 1988 - 1989 season that was especially good for the young player who scored 10 goals, was voted the PFA Young Player of the Year and made his debut in the England Under-21s. In September 1991, he won his first of 21 England caps when he appeared in a friendly against Germany.

Merson was in the very successful Arsenal side that won the 1991 League Championship, the League Cup and FA Cup in 1993 and the Cup Winners' Cup a year later. Despite his success he found himself in difficulty when he publicly admitted to having an addiction to drink and drugs, which resulted in the FA putting him on a three-month rehabilitation programme. He returned to Arsenal in February 1995.

After a short spell with relegated Middlesbrough, Merson signed for Aston Villa in late 1998 for £6.75m where his flamboyant style quickly established him as a firm favourite with the fans. He became club captain and was instrumental in five good years with Villa, reaching the FA Cup final in 2000, before he was given a free transfer to Portsmouth at the end of the 2001/2002 season helping his new team reach the Premier League in 2002/2003.

He then wanted a move and jumped at the chance to join Walsall in 2003, however, his gambling habit was disrupting his career and he sought professional help, but on his return to football, he found himself in the manager's position. The 2004/2005 campaign was difficult although 2005/2006 looked brighter, but Merson was sacked in February 2006 as the team failed to avoid relegation. He resumed his playing career for a brief spell with Tamworth and announced he was retiring from professional football in March 2006.

ACTIVE SEASONS:	1998/1999 to 2002/2003
APPEARANCES:	144
GOALS:	19

PAUL CELEBRATES WITH MARK DELANEY

MINGS

Tyrone Mings has risen from non-league to become captain of Aston Villa and a regular England international. The Bath born defender began his career at Yate Town and Chippenham Town, and played for Ipswich and Bournemouth before joining Villa on loan in January 2019.

He quickly became a fan's favourite and within six months was playing in the EFL Championship Play-Off final where he helped Villa defeat Derby 2-1 and gain promotion to the Premier League.

He signed for Villa permanently on 8 July 2019 and became captain following the departure of Jack Grealish to Manchester City in August 2021.

His consistent form for Villa earned him a senior England debut against Bulgaria in October 2019 and he was included in Gareth Southgate's squad for the UEFA Euro 2020 tournament playing in every match of the group stage.

On 15 November 2021 he scored his first England goal in a 10-0 away FIFA World Cup qualification victory over San Marino just weeks after passing the 100-match milestone for Villa.

TYRONE JUBILANT AFTER THE CHAMPIONSHIP PLAY-OFF FINAL VICTORY OVER DERBY COUNTY MAY 2019

TONY MORLEY (CENTRE) WITH GARY SHAW
AND WINNING GOALSCORER PETER WITHE
WITH THE EUROPEAN CUP, MAY 1982

RIGHT:
TONY MORLEY, 1980/81

MORLEY

Tony Morley in his heyday on the pitch was
a successful winger who gave his best years to Aston
Villa. He started his lifelong passion with football as
an apprentice at Preston North End in July 1969 and
became a professional in August 1972 and moved
to Burnley in February 1976 on a £100,000 transfer.
He joined Aston Villa for £200,000 in June 1979 where
he developed his dangerous skills under manager
Ron Saunders.

Morley became renowned for his spectacular goals and
possibly his most memorable coming in a game against
Everton at Goodison Park in Villa's successful 1980/1981
campaign. That goal was good enough to win the Goal of
the Season award. That season was also memorable for
Morley when he was an integral part of Villa's team that

won the League Championship, and the following year
would see the Villans win the European Cup, again with
a promising and steadfast Morley on the wing. Morley was
also part of the winning Villa side that claimed the
European Super Cup in 1983.

He established himself as a strong link in the Villa chain
and scored a total of 34 goals from his 180 appearances for
the club. Apart from his spectacular goals, was renowned
for his dribbling ability and crosses and was notoriously
fast on the wing. His shots were powerful, and he could
use both feet which gave the young player an advantage.

Morley was surprisingly transferred to rivals West Bromwich
Albion during the 1983 - 1984 campaign where his pace
and stoic playing went down well. However, he was loaned
to Birmingham City in late 1984 before he moved to Japan

to join FC Seiko in August 1985. The following year saw him move to Holland where he played for Den Haag before joining Walsall in 1987 and Notts County before heading back to The Hawthorns in August 1987.

After spells with a variety of clubs including Burnley (on loan October/ November 1988), Tampa Bay Rowdies in the US (1989), Sutton Town (1992) he briefly became a coach in both Australia and Hong Kong. Morley also assisted both Villa and West Bromwich Albion Old Stars during the 1990s. The devoted Villan won six caps for England but failed to be picked for any of the World Cup games in 1982 under manager Ron Greenwood. That decision seemed a bemusing one since Greenwood was all in favour of attacking players and Morley had exactly what the manager needed.

ACTIVE SEASONS:	**1979/1980 to 1983/1984**
APPEARANCES:	**180**
GOALS:	**34**

MORTIMER

It is often said that Dennis Mortimer must surely be one of the all-time greatest footballers who never won a cap for England. Nothing is really known about why this was the case, but Liverpool born Mortimer was the stalwart and driving force at Villa for 10 years.

His career began at Coventry City where he began as an apprentice in July 1967 and his promising midfield talents brought him to the attention of Villa manager Ron Saunders. Having worked his way up through the ranks at Coventry, Mortimer made more than 200 appearances for the Sky Blues, and he found the back of the net on 10 occasions.

He was signed for Villa in December 1975 for £175,000 where his passion and determination were developed to the full. His outstanding skills were combined with a driving force and the will to win. He was the backbone of the successful team between 1975 and 1985 and his 406 appearances for the club saw him score 36 goals. Mortimer found his niche between Des Bremner and Gordon Cowans who between them provided Villa with the right attitude to seek and find glory in the League Cup final in 1977. Further success came in 1981 with the First Division title while the European Cup and the European Super Cup were won over the next two seasons.

So impressive was Mortimer that Saunders was more than happy to give the captaincy to this exceptional midfielder. It was Mortimer that captained the side to glory in all of those three major trophies.

He was then loaned to Sheffield United in December 1984 during a clear-out of the playing squad and then moved to Brighton in August 1985. Following his spell with Brighton, Mortimer made the controversial move to Birmingham City in August 1986 before joining Kettering Town in July 1987. Redditch were pleased to snap him up as a player-manager between November 1987 and October 1988 while his next move took him to West Bromwich Albion as football in the community officer in August 1989. He later became the club's reserve team player and coach before he returned to the Villans as junior coach.

Although not particularly fitting for a player of his stature, Mortimer did win six Under-21 caps for England as well as three B-team places and six Under-23 caps, but that full debut alluded him.

ACTIVE SEASONS:	**1975/1976 to 1984/1985**
APPEARANCES:	**406**
GOALS:	**36**

NICHOLL

Chris Nicholl was a tall and commanding centre-back in his day and saw Villa through the bleak days of the Third Division to the heady days of the Saunders era and the top tier of English football.

English born Irish international Nicholl joined Villa in 1972 from Luton Town played an important part in Villa's renaissance during the 1970s, which saw him win two League Cup medals in 1975 and 1977.

In the latter final, which went to two replays, not only did Nicholl captain the Villa side but he scored one of the greatest goals any Villa fan has seen, a forty-yard left foot screamer which helped take the second reply into extra-time against Everton at Old Trafford.

On another occasion, Nicholl not only scored two rare goals for his own side, but also scored two own-goals for the opponents, Leicester City in a league game in 1976. Although Nicholl is the only top-flight English player to have done that, I believe it was done once before, in the lower divisions, but a very long time ago.

Following the League Cup victory in 1977, Nicholl was sold to Southampton in the summer and became the backbone of that successful side, playing in well over 220 appearances for the Saints. He later managed Southampton in June 1985 after Lawrie McMenemy resigned.

CHRIS NICHOLL IN ACTION DURING THE 1975 LEAGUE CUP FINAL WIN

BELOW:
CHRIS TACKLES EVERTON'S MARTIN DOBSON MARCH 1977

ACTIVE SEASONS:	1971/1972 to 1976/1977
APPEARANCES:	252
GOALS:	20

O'NEILL

Martin O'Neill came to Villa from Celtic in August 2006 on the back of an incredible spell at Celtic Park, where he managed the 'Hoops' to win 75% of their games, a club record. He'd had previous success in the Premier League with Leicester before he joined Celtic, and got the Foxes promoted and won the League Cup in 1997 and 2000, as well as reaching the final in 1999.

He joined Villa on the back of the takeover by Randy Lerner in 2006, bringing a new era to Villa Park, a bold and bright era, with the slogan, "Proud History, Bright Future", where the club were aiming to compete with the Premier League 'big boys'. It all started very well for O'Neill, with Villa unbeaten for the first nine league games of the season, but they suffered a mid-season slump, then finished the season with another nine games unbeaten to finish 11th.

During the next season, there was speculation O'Neill was to be offered the England manager's position, but this was pure conjecture and nothing materialised. Villa finished 6th in his second season and qualified for the Inter-Toto Cup.

During that season, Villa scored a club record 71 goals in the Premier League. During the 2008/2009 season, Villa were on 51 points after 25 games and on course for a top-four finish; however, having qualified for the UEFA Cup, O'Neill upset Villa fans by fielding an under-strength side in the European competition against CSKA Moscow and they lost. The reason given was that O'Neill wanted to prioritise the Premier League over Europe. Following that UEFA Cup defeat, Villa failed to win any of the next eight games and so failed to reach the top-four, but still finished 6th again and qualified for the Europa League.

After failing to qualify for the Europa League group stages in 2009/2010, they finished 6th for the third season in a row under O'Neill with 64 points (Villa's highest Premier League points total). Villa reached the 2010 League Cup Final but lost 2-1 to Manchester United.

A few days before the start of the 2010/2011 season, Martin O'Neill stunned the football world, and upset Villa fans again by walking out on the club, unhappy at the lack of funds available to strengthen the squad for the forthcoming season. The rest is history.

MARTIN O'NEILL PROUDLY HOLDS UP A VILLA SHIRT AS HE IS UNVEILED AS MANAGER IN 2006

PETROV

Stiliyan Petrov, better known to his teammates and fans as 'Stan' is a living legend at the Villa, not only for his playing career at the club but because of his brave fight against cancer.

Born in Bulgaria, Petrov joined Celtic from CSKA Sofia in 1999 and stayed with the club until he moved to the Villa in 2006 along with Martin O'Neill. He later became club captain while also playing 106 matches for the Bulgarian national side.

Powerful and influential in the middle of the park, Petrov drove the team on week after week and he also scored his fair share of goals. He started his career at Villa as an anchor-man, protecting the defence, in the centre of midfield, but the 2011/2012 season saw him handed more license to thrill, as he did every week at Celtic - and Villa reaped the rewards.

In March 2012, Petrov was diagnosed with acute leukaemia suspending his football career to have treatment and he announced his retirement from the game in May 2013. During that final season, the Villa fans marked his retirement by a round of heart-felt clapping in the 19th minute of each home game, 19 being the number on his shirt.

Since retiring from playing, spent a time as assistant coach of the Aston Villa Under-21 squad, working alongside another former villa player, Gordon Cowans. During the summer of 2016, Petrov trained with Villa in order to earn a contract and played during pre-season matches but was not offered a playing contract by manager Roberto Di Matteo.

ACTIVE SEASONS:	2006/2007 to 2011/2012
APPEARANCES:	219
GOALS:	12

PLATT

David Platt became one of Villa's most prolific midfielders in recent history and was adored by the Villa faithful.

He joined Crewe Alexandra where he earned a solid reputation as a scoring midfielder where he played in 134 league appearances at Crewe and scored 56 goals, Signed by Graham Taylor for £200,000 while Villa were in Division Two, Platt scored 68 goals in 155 league and cup games for Villa and he earned his first cap for England, under Bobby Robson, in 1989 in a friendly against Italy.

Despite being a versatile and reliable player, he often found himself on the England bench initially. However, Platt was picked on occasions for England, and gave a particularly memorable performance in the World Cup 1990 when he started in a quarter-final tie against Cameroon. It was Platt who scored the opening goal in what was to be an exciting 3 - 2 victory for England after striking a superb volley on the turn in the match against Belgium. Platt finished his England career in 1996 with a hefty 27 goals in 62 appearances that included 19 occasions when he captained his country.

Platt was an exceptional player for Villa during the early 1990s and captained the team providing leadership and inspiration and scored many goals from his position in midfield. In 1991 he left Villa for Italy where he joined Bari for £5.5m, followed by spells at Juventus and Sampdoria, but moved back to England four years later when he signed for Arsenal. Platt played with the London club for three years and was part of the 1998 Arsenal team that won the Premier League and FA Cup double before his retirement in 1998. Platt served as manager of Sampdoria before leaving his post owing to poor results. Afterwards, he returned to England again as player-manager of Nottingham Forest followed by a spell managing the England Under-21 team and was later part of the management team at Manchester City between 2010 and 2013 under his former teammate, Roberto Mancini.

DAVID PLATT IN CLARET AND BLUE, 1991/92

ACTIVE SEASONS:	**1987/1988 to 1990/1991**
APPEARANCES:	**155**
GOALS:	**68**

PREMIER LEAGUE

With the advent of the FA Premier League in 1992, when Villa were again a founder member, they finished runners-up to Manchester United in the inaugural season of 1992/1993. Since those heady days under Ron Atkinson, Villa have failed to finish that high in the Premier League again, although they have managed 4th and 5th on one occasion each and 6th placed finishes on five occasions.

Having spent 24 years in the Premier League, the club were relegated at the end of the 2015/2016 season and spent three seasons in the Championship (second tier), until winning the Championship Play-Off final on 27th May 2019.

The manager who bought them up, Dean Smith, a boyhood Villa fan was sacked in early November 2021 just 11 games into the Premier League season after struggling to fill the gap left by Jack Grealish's transfer to Manchester City in the summer. His replacement was the Liverpool and England legend Steven Gerrard, who in his first managerial post revitalised Rangers and regained the Scottish title from Celtic after a decade of playing second-fiddle. The appointment was a major coup for the Villa and will greatly help them attract the very top players to the club as they continue their quest for a top-four Premier League finish.

QUINTESSENTIAL VILLA

In this section, there are some Villa facts and figures that every Villa fan should know.

107 seasons in the top tier of English football (up until the 2020/2021 season).

Aston Villa v Everton is the most played fixture in English football.

Villa have the 5th most major honours (20) won by an English club.

128 goals were scored by Villa in the 1930/1931 league season, a record that still stands in the top-flight.

Charlie Aitken still holds the record appearances as a Villa player, 660.

Three Villa players have won the PFA Players' Player of the Year: Andy Gray (1977), David Platt (1990), Paul McGrath (1993).

The 1982 Villa team that won the European Cup were inducted in the English Football Hall of Fame.

There have been 33 Aston Villa managers.

Josef Vengloš was the very first foreign (non-UK) manager to manage a top-flight English club in 1990.

Sir Doug Ellis acquired the name 'Deadly Doug' from legend, Jimmy Greaves while on a fishing trip together. Jimmy apparently saw Doug knock a salmon on the head after he'd caught it. Another theory was because of his penchant hiring and firing of managers - he fired 13 managers during his chairmanship.

Roberto Di Matteo lasted only 12 games and served the shortest term as a Villa manager.

76 Villa players (as of 2021) have been capped for England, second only to Tottenham.

Current England manager, Gareth Southgate is the most capped Villa player (42 England caps while a Villa player).

Olof Mellberg is the most capped international player with 69 caps for Sweden.

Aston Villa were founder members of both the Football League (1888) and the Premier League (in 1992).

During the 1937/1938 season, 1.1 million fans watched their team at Villa Park.

Villa were relegated from the top tier for the first time in the club's history in the 1935/1936 season.

Gerry Hitchens scored five goals in a game when Villa beat Charlton 11-1 at Villa Park on 14th November 1959. It was also Villa's highest post-War victory.

The most fans to attend a Villa game (officially 121,919) was against Sunderland on 19th April 1913 in the FA Cup Final at The Crystal Palace, although that figure included all the other people admitted to the Crystal Palace that day for other activities.

George Best once played for Villa ...for 60 minutes anyway. He played in fundraiser event at Villa Park in aid of the Bradford City stadium disaster in 1985.

Villa Park has played host to more FA Cup semi-finals than any other club ground.

Gerry Hitchens is the most prolific post-War goal-scorer with a goal every 1.6 games (96 goals in 160 appearances for Villa).

Billy Walker holds the best scoring record in a Villa shirt with 244 league and cup goals.

Harry Hampton holds the record for the most hat-tricks for Villa (14).

'Pongo' Waring holds the record number of goals in a season with 50 league and cup goals in 40 appearances in the 1930/1931 season.

On 27th February 1999, the last all-English-born team was fielded in the English top-flight when Villa played Coventry City. That team was: Oakes, Watson, Southgate, Scimeca, Wright, Taylor, Merson, Grayson, Hendrie, Dublin, Joachim. Even the subs were English: Barry, Draper, Collymore.

Villa's European Cup winner, Peter Withe used to receive a bag of sweets after every game from a lady supporter in the Witton Lane Stand.

Savo Milošević was signed from Partizan Belgrade by Brian Little after he watched videos of him and he hadn't scouted him live.

Chris Nicholl once scored four goals in one game against Leicester City - two for each team.

Jack Grealish's great, great grandfather was a Villa player called Billy Garraty who was a forward and played 260 games for the Villans and scored 112 goals between 1897 and 1908. He helped Villa win the FA Cup in 1905. He also made one appearance for England.

Villa once beat local rivals Small Heath (now Birmingham City) 22-0 in the 1870s.

Aston Villa caused an international stir on a tour of pre-World War II Germany when the team refused to give Adolf Hitler the Nazi salute. The German leader was unaccustomed to such an insult as other British teams had complied.

Villa Park hosted the very last European Cup Winners' Cup Final in 1999 between Mallorca and Lazio.

Villa were European Champions in May 1982 but on 27th December 1982 they lost 3=0 to Birmingham City, who were rock bottom of the First Division - how can that happen?

PETER WITHE SCORES VS CHELSEA AT VILLA PARK, SEPTEMBER 1984

RAMPANT LION

In October 1878, four years after Aston Villa FC had been formed, the club introduced an official badge which was displayed on their shirts.

The introduction of the 'Rampant Lion' logo and the word 'Prepared' was first seen during the 1878/1879 season, but apparently the lion was facing in a different direction to today's lion.

The logo was brought into existence by the then club Secretary, George Ramsay and William McGregor, who were both Scottish, hence adopting the lion symbol. However, the logo didn't last long on the shirts as it was too large and didn't re-appear until the 1956/1957 season, the year Villa won the FA Cup.

Since 1957, there have been several iterations (eight in fact) of the lion badge, with the latest coming only a few years ago, in 2016 when the lion was reshaped with more prominent claws and enlarged. The word 'Prepared' was also removed to the annoyance of some of the fans.

2016 - Present

2007-2016

2000-2007

1992-2000

1973-1992

1969-1973

1956-1969

1874-1886

RAMSAY

George Ramsay started at Villa when the club was a mere parks team, and by the time he left, they were a 'Super Team', a club that had achieved much greatness during that time.

Aston Villa Wesleyan Chapel FC (the former name of Aston Villa FC) were playing a practice match in Aston Park in 1875 and a 21-year-old George Ramsay asked if he could join the game. Although the other players were not convinced about Ramsay and whether he should join in, he was allowed to play as one of the sides were on man short. To everyone's surprise, Ramsay showed off his skills and ball control and he was immediately appointed captain for the day. From that day on, he became a Villa player.

Ramsay was a leader on and off the field and during the course of the next five years, he led his team to their first trophy win, the Birmingham Senior Cup in 1880, and later that year, they won the FA Cup for the first time. His philosophy was to attack the opposition by passing the ball around the field and trying to score at every opportunity.

Ramsay suffered an injury in that same year (1880) that caused him to retire from playing, but he remained active at the club, and in 1886 he became the club secretary (the modern-day version would be the Director of Football).

He remained in post for the next 40 years!

During that time, he played a huge contribution in making Villa probably the very first 'Super Club' in the country and helped the club win SIX Championships and SIX FA Cups.

He was simply, Villa's greatest and most successful ever manager.

SAUNDERS
RON

Ron Saunders had a distinguished playing career before his successful managerial career. He was a prolific striker for Everton, Gillingham, Watford and Charlton, but it was at Portsmouth he had the most success, scoring 162 goals in 261 games between 1958 and 1964 and remains the club's third-highest goal-scorer still to this day.

Saunders began his managerial career at Yeovil Town in 1967, then went to Oxford for one season before becoming Norwich manager, where he had some success in guiding them to promotion to the Second Division title in 1971/1972 and losing finalists of the League Cup in 1973. However, in the same year he had a row with the board of directors and resigned. He joined Manchester City five days after resigning at Norwich and steered them to the League Cup Final, but they lost to Wolves. Saunders was dismissed just before the end of the 1973/1974 season and joined Villa, who were in the Second Division.

At Villa, he guided the club out of the second tier as runners-up in his first season and also won the League Cup in the same year, and in doing that, became the first manager to guide three different clubs to successive League Cup finals. He quickly established Villa as a top First Division club and managed the club to another League Cup trophy in 1977. However, his biggest triumph was achieved in the 1980/1981 season when he guided Villa to their first Championship for 71 years.

RON SAUNDERS
ACKNOWLEDGES
THE FANS, 2006

Saunders surprisingly resigned in February 1982, just as the club were embarking on a remarkable run in the European Cup, and by the time he resigned, they had reached the quarter-finals. Tony Barton took over as manager and steered the Villans to the final and beyond.

In a move that enraged Villa fans, he joined local rivals Birmingham City, but they were relegated in 1984, but he got them back up at the first attempt. In 1986 he walked out on the club and took charge of West Bromwich Albion, where he wasn't able to stop the Baggies from being relegated into the Second Division. He was later sacked after failing to get them promoted back. That was his last managerial position.

Following his retirement, Saunders seemed reluctant to return to Villa Park as a spectator and was rarely seen there, in fact the first time he'd returned was in 1994 for a testimonial for Tony Barton when he managed a Villa side made up of mainly the European Cup team. In 2006, his next appearance, he was 'guest of honour' for a game against Manchester United, invited by the new owner, Randy Lerner. He also returned for the 25th anniversary of the European Cup victory in May 2007.

Ron Saunders passed away on 7th December 2019 aged 87 after a long illness. He will always be fondly remembered by the fans as Villa's most successful post-War manager.

SHAW

Gary Shaw exploded on the scene in the early 1980s. The Brummie-born striker began his football career with the club as an apprentice in July 1977 making his debut in a game against Bristol City in August 1978.

He turned professional in 1979 and struck up a fabulous partnership with Peter Withe, managing to find the back of the net on 20 occasions (in all competitions) during the Championship-winning 1980/1981 season and was voted PFA Young Player of the Year. In the following season the sensational striker's form continued as he scored 14 times. In that 1981 – 1982 season, he was an integral part of the Villa side that won both the European Cup (1982) and the European super Cup (1983). The former resulted in Shaw being named the European Cup's Player of the Year but the fairy-tale was not to last.

Sadly, he suffered a serious knee injury during the 1983/1984 campaign which was to effectively ended his career. He underwent a staggering six operations to rectify the problem, but his promising start at Villa was over. He tried his luck abroad following the surgery and moved first to Copenhagen and then Klagenfurt in Austria upon leaving Villa Park at the end of the 1987/1988 season.

Shaw failed to make any league appearances for either club and returned to England and a short spell with Walsall in 1990. The same year saw him try his luck with Kilmarnock where his four league appearances resulted in no goals.

He then joined Shrewsbury Town later that year and over the following season made 22 league appearances which saw him score on five occasions for the club. Finding the stress on his knee too great, Shaw retired from football in 1991 and the tender age of just 30 years old.

Earlier in his career when his goalscoring was prolific, Shaw had come to the attention of the England Under-21 squad, winning seven caps, although he never won a full cap for England.

What a talent he was, and what he could have been is something every Villa fan of a certain age will always think about - he was the 'golden boy' of football in the early 1980s, and an unfulfilled talent for sure.

ACTIVE SEASONS:	1978/1979 to 1987/1988
APPEARANCES:	213
GOALS:	79

SOUTHGATE

Gareth Southgate had an illustrious career and played 242 times for Villa, before becoming a manager.

He joined Villa from Crystal Palace on 23rd June 1995 for a then Villa as a record of £2.5m signed by Brian Little. He was initially signed as a midfielder, although he'd played for Palace as a right-back as well, but Little quickly saw his strength as a centre-back and formed a formidable partnership with Ugo Ehiogu and Paul McGrath. In his first season he helped his side lift the League Cup in 1996 and Villa qualified for the UEFA Cup. He became captain in the 1997 – 1998 season following the departure of Andy Townsend and then steered Villa to the 2000 FA Cup final against Chelsea, but that ended in defeat.

Just before Euro 2000, Southgate handed in a transfer request to manager John Gregory, claiming "it was time to move on", a statement that didn't endear him to the Villa faithful and was eventually transferred to Middlesbrough on 11th July 2001 for £6.5m.

Southgate was capped 57 times by England, 42 of them while a Villa player before his playing career ended in May 2006 at the age of 35, and after more than 500 league appearances. He was appointed Middlesbrough manager, a position held until 2009 prior to being made England Under-21 job.

I won't mention what happened at Wembley in 1996.

Southgate was elevated to senior England manager in 2016 and is still in that post to this day.

**GARETH SOUTHGATE
1999/2000**

LEFT:
GARETH BATTLES WITH MANCHESTER UNITED'S NICKY BUTT,

ACTIVE SEASONS:	1995/1996 to 2000/2001
APPEARANCES:	242
GOALS:	9

SPINK

Another highly regarded former goalkeeper for Aston Villa was Nigel Spink. He began his career in the youth teams of West Ham United in 1976 and then Chelmsford City (1976 - 1977) before being signed by Ron Saunders in January 1977 for £4,000 as an 18-year-old.

However, Spink had to be patient and had to wait for five years for his big break, and he couldn't have dreamt for a bigger stage to announce himself, as he came on as a substitute in the 1982 European Cup final in Rotterdam. First-choice 'keeper Jimmy Rimmer was injured in the ninth minute of the game against Bayern Munich and Spink's big chance had arrived unexpectedly.

NIGEL IN FULL FLIGHT, 1993/94

What a chance for the tall 'keeper, and he didn't waste his opportunity and made the game his own, kept a clean sheet and helped Villa win the final 1-0.

Having kept a clean sheet in the biggest game of all, Spink had to wait another year before he claimed the number one jersey was his to keep, but when he did, he kept it for the next 10 years, until the arrival of another Villa legend in Mark Bosnich. He was capped by England once in 1983 and twice by England B in 1991.

Having been at Villa Park for almost two decades and
playing in 460 games, Spink headed for West Bromwich
Albion in 1996 where he stayed for a year. Millwall
(1997/2000) was his next stop before he signed for Forest
Green Rovers in 2000. He made 14 appearances for his
final club before hanging up his boots in 2001 at the age
of almost 42.

Spink's excellent reputation on the pitch was well-founded.
He was a good shot-stopper, tall at 6' 2" and was always
calm and prepared for any challenge the opposition could
kick or head at him. His confident style combined with his
courage and sound anticipation made him a firm Villa
favourite.

After retiring from playing, Spink became a manager at
Forest Green Rovers in the Conference National League
for two years and led them to the 2001 FA Trophy final, but
they fell short, losing 1-0 to Canvey Island, ironically played
at Villa Park. He was sacked in September 2002.

Following his brief spell as manager, he joined Steve
Bruce's coaching team at Birmingham City, Wigan and
Sunderland as a goalkeeping coach but left the last post
at the Stadium of Light in February 2011 where he went
spent a few months at Bristol City until he quit football to
start up a courier business.

ACTIVE SEASONS:	1981/1982 to 1995/1996
APPEARANCES:	460
GOALS:	0

TAYLOR

Graham Taylor became a footballer in 1962 and spent 10 years playing for only two clubs - Grimsby Town and Lincoln City, before retiring in 1972 through injury. He stayed with Lincoln after hanging up his boots and managed them for five years before moving to Watford in 1976. At Lincoln they won the Division Four championship under his watch.

At Watford, he became a legend after taking them from Division Four all the way to the top tier in five years. In fact, he got them so close to winning the Division One title in the 1982/1983 season, finishing runners-up and also, they were losing finalist in the 1984 FA Cup.

After Villa were relegated in the 1986/1987 season, Graham Taylor was appointed Villa manager and had no qualms about the job he had just taken on. He pulled no punched and stated the club needed root and branch change and described the team as "as shambles".

That Villa team Taylor inherited, included four of the 1982 European Cup squad, the likes of Gary Shaw, Allan Evans, Andy Blair, Nigel Spink and he led them to promotion as runners-up at the first attempt. The key recruit to the team was an unknown player called David Platt from Crewe.

Back in the top-tier, Taylor recruited heavily but only just managed to avoid relegation in the 1988/1989 campaign. However, the following season was the complete opposite, and with the addition of two big central defenders in Kent Neilsen and Paul McGrath, Villa finished runners-up to Liverpool and reached the quarter-final of the FA Cup.

With Taylor's pedigree increasing by then, the FA came calling following Bobby Robson's resignation after the 1990 World Cup and they appointed Taylor as England manager, in a role that was said to be "The Impossible Job".

The England job ended up being too big for Taylor and although he lasted three years, he decided to go back into

club management with Wolves and then back to Watford in 1996. His second spell with the Hornets finished with relegation after only one season in the Premier League and they parted company for the second time.

In 2001, Taylor was appointed into a non-executive director role at Villa under Doug Ellis and when John Gregory left in January 2002, Taylor was appointed as his successor.

Just like at Watford, he was not so successful the second time around and decided to quit after the 2002/2003 season.

He sadly passed away on 12th January 2017 at the age of 72. Graham Taylor was one of football's gentlemen, a lovely man and cared passionately about his players, something that can't be said about some football managers.

GRAHAM UNVEILED AS THE NEW ASTON VILLA, FEBRUARY 2002

TOWNSEND

Andy Townsend began his career with Welling United youth team in 1980 and remained dedicated to the club for four years before turning professional and signing for Weymouth in 1984.

ANDY TOWNSEND CELEBRATES COCA COLA CUP VICTORY OVER LEEDS UNITED WITH THE TROPHY, MARCH 1996

The English-born Irish midfielder moved to Southampton a year later where he made 71 league appearances and scored a total of eight goals. He was signed by Lawrie McMenemy for £35,000 and ironically, made his debut against Aston Villa in April 1985. Chris Nicholl took over the helm at the Saints and Townsend found himself in and out of the team, but disaster struck when in a friendly against his former club Weymouth, Townsend broke his leg in 1986. By January 1987 he was back in the first team having regained his fitness and he became a regular alongside Glenn Cockerill and Jimmy Case in midfield.

Nicholl then sold Townsend to Norwich City for £300,000 in August 1988 where he remained until 1990 when he moved to Chelsea, but it was his success at Norwich that earned Townsend a place in the Irish squad and eventually earned over 70 caps. A year earlier in July 1993, in a transfer of just over £2 million, the midfielder moved to Villa, and it was there he made his name and went on

to help the team win the League Cup final against Manchester United in 1994, and he then captained the Villa team who claimed the trophy in a 3-0 win over Leeds United two years later.

Townsend joined Middlesbrough in August 1997 for £500,000 and made 37 appearances for his new club while 'Boro won promotion into the Premier League. He established a steady partnership with Paul Gascoigne in the 1998/1999 campaign but the following season saw him fighting for a place in the first team. in 1999 he transferred to West Bromwich Albion where he made 17 league appearances.

Disappointingly for Townsend a persistent knee injury meant the end of his playing days and he retired from professional football in July 2000.

He is now a regular television and radio pundit.

ACTIVE SEASONS:	1993/1994 to 1997/1998
APPEARANCES:	176
GOALS:	11

UGO

Ugo Ehiogu started his career as a trainee at West Bromwich Albion before becoming a professional in 1989. The then Villa manager, Ron Atkinson paid £40,000 for his services in August 1991, and it was money well worth spending. By 1994 he had replaced Shaun Teale in the heart of the Villa defence and formed a partnership with both Paul McGrath and Gareth Southgate.

He was a gangling but commanding figure in the Villa defence and remained at the club for nine years, and helped Villa win the League Cup in 1996 and was on the losing side when Villa played Chelsea in the 2000 FA Cup Final. He joined Middlesbrough in November 2000 and won the League Cup with them in 2004. Ugo also played briefly for Leeds United (on loan), Rangers and Sheffield United, before ending his playing career in 2009.

He was the first black player to captain the England Under-21 team in 1993 and won four England caps and scored once for his country.

UGO EHIOGU, 1999/00

Ugo sadly died of a cardiac arrest on 21st April 2017 while was at the Tottenham Hotspur training ground where he was a was the Under-23 coach. He will always be a Villa legend. A picture of Ugo can be seen in the corner of the Holte End stand to remind fans of his greatness as a man and a footballer.

ACTIVE SEASONS:	1991/1992 to 2000/2001
APPEARANCES:	302
GOALS:	15

VILLA PARK

Aston Villa have used various grounds to play football matches, including Aston Park, Wellington Road, Perry Barr before settling at Villa Park in 1897. Indeed, they also played home games at Aston Lower Grounds, a Victorian amusement park that would in the very near future become transformed into Villa Park.

The club had settled at Perry Barr in 1876 but found that they needed a larger home as the team's popularity grew and they succeeded on the pitch. In fact, when Villa played Preston North End in the fifth round of the 1887/1888 FA Cup more than 27,000 spectators turned up to watch the match. As kick-off time approached, the police realised that they didn't have enough manpower on duty to control the crowd and they had to call on soldiers stationed nearby to help restore order after spectators wanting to get a better view had twice encroached on the pitch.

The playing surface had been destroyed by the crowd and the mounted police, so the two team captains agreed to play the match as a friendly which the visitors won 3-1.

However, the FA later backed Preston's claim to victory, citing that Villa could not replay the game as it was their fault, they couldn't maintain order.

Some things never change!

Villa spent £20,000 on a new ground which they named Villa Park with a capacity of 70,000. The first game to be played there was a league fixture against Blackburn Rovers and the home fans went home in buoyant spirits having seen their side win 3/0.

Villa Park has seen plenty of redevelopment over the years with the cycle track being removed in 1914 so that the Witton Lane stand could be enlarged and the famous Holte End banking - named after the owner of Aston Hall to whom the land had previously belonged - was completed at the end of 1939. It was the decision to use Villa Park as a venue for the 1966 World Cup that brought major transformation with the pitch being extended, the Witton Lane stand being made all-seater, and seats being introduced to the Witton End banking behind the goal.

The North Stand was built in the late 1970s to replace the Witton End banking while the Witton Lane stand was rebuilt two decades later and renamed the Doug Ellis Stand. The famous Holte End terracing remained until the Taylor Report recommended all-seater stadia in England, so the stand was demolished in 1994 and rebuilt in the same Victorian red-brick style as the old Trinity Road Stand.

The new millennium saw the completion of the Trinity Road Stand (which replaced the previous structure built in the 1920s).

The club had initial planning permission in the Randy Lerner era to rebuild the North Stand in the same style as the Trinity Road Stand and the Holte End which would have increased capacity to over 50,000 (currently 42,785) but is yet to develop that stand; however, it is thought the new multi-millionaire owners hope to develop the North Stand to include a museum, sooner rather than later.

Villa Park has hosted some important events in its time, including England internationals, 1966 World Cup group games, 1996 European Championship games, numerous FA Cup semi-finals and the very last European Cup Winners' Cup Final in 1999, as well as several rock concerts and even rugby matches and NFL games.

VILLA PARK LOOKING MAGNIFICENT BEFORE THE PREMIER LEAGUE CLASH WITH WEST HAM UNITED, OCTOBER 2021

WALKER

Billy Walker was arguably, the most outstanding footballer ever to don the claret and blue shirt of Aston Villa.

The inside-forward made his Villa debut in an FA Cup game against QPR in January 1920 and scored a brace. At the end of that FA Cup campaign, he collected a winners' medal; not a bad first season, scoring 13 goals in 21 league and cup games.

Walker captained Villa for six seasons from 1926 and was capped 18 times for England spanning 12 years, in a day when international games were few and far between.

He was a one-club wonder, and had an incredible record, playing 531 games for Villa and scoring 244 goals, and was part of that Villa side who finished runners-up to Arsenal in the 1930/1931 season when Villa scored a record 128 top-flight goals, with Walker contributing 15 at the grand old age of 33.

He retired from playing in 1933, when he became manager of Sheffield Wednesday, Chelmsford City and Nottingham Forest. He was successful too, winning the FA Cup with both Wednesday (1935) and Forest (1959), among other honours. He became the only manager to win the FA Cup before and after the War. He retired from management in 1960 at the grand old age of 62.

ACTIVE SEASONS:	1919/1920 to 1933/1934
APPEARANCES:	531
GOALS:	244

WARING

Simply put, Tom 'Pongo' Waring was an enigma and will always be a Villa legend. Villa's record goal-scorer in a single season with **49** league goals in the **1930/1931** season was a law unto himself, turning up for training when he wanted but the Villa Park faithful loved him because he was a scoring machine. In a total of **225** appearances, he found the back of the net on **167** occasions ...an incredible record of consistency.

He was nicknamed "Pongo" after a popular cartoon of the inter-War years and was also known as 'the Gay Cavalier' for his goalscoring exploits. He joined Villa from Tranmere Rovers for the princely sum of £4,700 in February 1928. His five-year spell at Villa wrote his name in the record books and he is probably the greatest striker ever to have worn the claret and blue shirt.

'Pongo' joined Barnsley in November 1935 and the move angered fans so much that thousands of them demanded for his return but to no avail. He also played for Wolves, Tranmere (again), Accrington Stanley, Bath City, Ellesmere Port Town, Graysons FC, Birkenhead Dockers and Harrowby before guesting for New Brighton as the second World War began. He was capped five times by England (scoring four goals) between 1931 and 1932.

Waring worked for the Hercules Motor and Cycle Company in Aston following his retirement from football and died on 20 December 1980, aged 74.

TOM 'PONGO' WARING IN ACTION AGAINST TOTTENHAM HOTSPUR'S FRED CHANNELL

ACTIVE SEASONS:	1927/1928 to 1935/1936
APPEARANCES:	225
GOALS:	167

Withe was a showman and at the end of every home match he used to collect a bag of sweets from a lady in the stands, sometimes in exchange for one of his famous sweatbands.

By the time Withe left for Sheffield United in 1985 he'd scored 92 goals for Villa. Withe was a well-travelled footballer, having played for no less than 14 clubs, including time spent in South Africa and the United States.

WITHE

Peter Withe will always be remembered by Villa fans for scoring the winning goal in the 1982 European Cup Final, but he did so much more than that for Villa.

Liverpudlian, Withe was described by Villa manager, Ron Saunders as the "final piece in the jigsaw" when he paid £500,000 (a then Villa club record) from Newcastle for the much-travelled striker in 1980. And it was money worth spending.

Within two years, Withe had formed a lethal partnership with Gary Shaw and scored 20 league goals in the club's Championship winning campaign of 1980/1981 and scoring the winning goal in the European Cup Final a year later and featured in the European Super Cup win over Barcelona in 1983. Those three seasons capped a glorious chapter in the history of Aston Villa.

He was also part of Brian Clough's successful Nottingham Forest team between 1976 and 1978. He played for his beloved England 11 times and scored one goal.

After his playing career, he briefly became Villa's assistant manager under Jo Venglos. Withe then became manager of Wimbledon in October 1991 but that wasn't particularly successful after only winning one game and was replaced after just over 100 days.

After another spell with Villa as Youth Team Development under Ron Atkinson, he went into football management again with the Thailand national team and the Indonesian national team and was successful during his time in Asia.

PETER SCORES AGAINST EVERTON AT VILLA PARK, FEBRUARY 1983

ACTIVE SEASONS:	1980/1981 to 1984/1985
APPEARANCES:	233
GOALS:	92

GORDON COWANS

BELOW:
PAUL MCGRATH BATTLES WITH DAVID BATTY
AT ST JAMES' PARK, APRIL 1996

X FACTOR

Aston Villa have had some outstanding players don the famous claret and blue shirt over the years. Everyone has their favourites, but in 2006, at the start of a new era for the club when Randy Lerner took over the running of the club from Sir Doug Ellis, a list of 12 Villa icons was drawn up from fans' votes and they entered the club's first ever 'Aston Villa Hall of Fame'.

THE 12 ICONS WERE:

Gordon Cowans

Eric Houghton (player and manager)

Brian Little (player and manager)

Dennis Mortimer

Ron Saunders (manager)

Peter Withe

Paul McGrath

Peter McParland

Charlie Aitken

William McGregor (director)

George Ramsay (player and Club Secretary)

Billy Walker

In May 2013, Stillyan Petrov was added.

ALLAN EVANS, DENNIS MORTIMER AND
KENNY SWAIN WITH THE EUROPEAN CUP, MAY 1982

BELOW:
GRAHAM TAYLOR

In addition to the club's own Hall of Fame, The National
Football Museum in Manchester administers an 'English
Football Hall of Fame' and that currently includes one
Villa team, five ex-Villa players, two Villa managers and
a director.

THAT LIST INCLUDES:

The 1982 European Cup team

Clem Stephenson

Danny Blanchflower

Peter Schmeichel

Paul McGrath

Cyrille Regis

Joe Mercer (manager)

Graham Taylor (manager)

William McGregor (founder of the Football League)

YORKE

Striker Dwight Yorke made such an impression on Villa manager Graham Taylor during the club's **1989** tour of the West Indies that the unknown youngster was offered a trial at the club. Born in Canaan, Tobago, Yorke arrived at Villa Park and made such an impact that he was offered a contract after the trial.

Although he made two substitute appearances for Villa in his first season, it wasn't until the following campaign that he began to get a regular run in the first team and that was obviously helped by his first goal in English football, in a 3-2 victory over Derby County in February 1991.

Yorke initially started his Villa career on the right wing but was moved to spearhead the attack in 1995/1996 with immediate results and he netted a total of 61 goals in 131 appearances over the next three seasons and scored important goals to help his side lift the League Cup in 1996 and reach the quarter-final of the UEFA Cup two years later. Yorke spent 10 seasons with Villa, and it was this sort of goal return that persuaded Manchester United to shell out £12.6 million for his services in August 1998, and led Villa manager, John Gregory to quip, "If I'd had a gun, I would have shot him..."

It was at Old Trafford that the Trinidad and Tobago international really found his goalscoring form with 47 goals in 95 games and he helped the club to a hat-trick of Premier League titles. The 1998/1999 season was outstanding though, with United claiming the League, FA Cup and European Cup to complete a treble that has never been equalled before or since. However, the arrival of Dutchman, Ruud van Nistelrooy signalled the end for Yorke, and he joined Blackburn Rovers in 2002 for £2 million.

His time at Ewood Park was full of ups and downs but a falling out with manager Graeme Souness led to a free transfer to join former United team-mate Steve Bruce at Birmingham City in 2004. Despite scoring on his debut, Yorke spent much of the season on the bench and departed for Australia the following year.

Playing for Sydney FC, Yorke proved a worthwhile signing and helped the club to the A-league Grand Final before announcing his intention to join Championship side Sunderland. Yorke again teamed up with a former Manchester United star in manager Roy Keane and was instrumental in helping the Black Cats return to the top-flight at the first attempt.

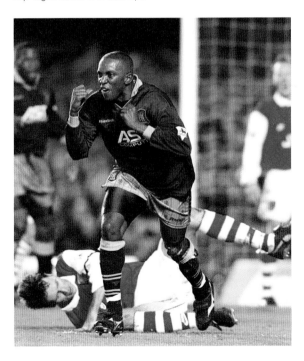

ACTIVE SEASONS:	1989/1990 to 1998/1999
APPEARANCES:	287
GOALS:	98

ALPAY OZALAN

Z-LIST

Aston Villa have played quite a few teams that include the letter 'Z' in their name, and not surprisingly all played in European competitions.

The matches Villa have played against teams that included 'z' in their names were as follows:

Górnik Zabrze from Poland
in the 1977/1978 UEFA Cup 2nd Round

Internazionale Milano from Italy
in the 1990/1991 UEFA Cup 2nd Round

Internazionale Milano from Italy
in the 1994/1995 UEFA Cup 1st Round

Trabzonspor from Turkey
in the 1994/1995 UEFA Cup 2nd Round

FC Zürich from Switzerland
in the 2002 Inter Toto Cup 3rd Round

MSK Žilina from Slovakia
in the 2008/2009 UEFA Cup Group Stages

Aston Villa played in a competition called the Zenith Data Systems Cup (formerly called the the Simod Cup) in 1989/1990 and 1991/1992.

In the 1989/1990 season, Villa lost in the Northern Area Final 4-2 over two legs to Middlesbrough. Two seasons later, Villa lost to Nottingham Forest in the 3rd Round. The competition only lasted three seasons in its name.

Surprisingly, there have been more than several players who have played for Villa whose names have included the letter 'z' or come from countries with 'z' in the name.

The list includes the following:

Zambians, Freddie Mwila and Emment Kapengwe
played briefly for Aston Villa in the 1969/1970 season, making four appearances between them.

Tanzanian striker, Mbwana Samatta
was signed for Aston Villa in 2020.

Alpay Ozalan
played for Villa between 2000 and 2004.

John McKenzie
was a Scot who played for Villa between 1908 & 1909.

Thomas Hitzlsperger
was a German international who played for Villa between 2000 and 2005.

Walter Hazelden
played for Villa between 1957 and 1959.

BRAD GUZAN

LEFT:
THOMAS HITZLSPERGER

Brad Guzan
was an American goalkeeper who played for Villa between 2008 and 2016.

Ulises De la Cruz
played for Villa between 2002 and 2006.

Matthias Breitkreutz
was a German midfielder who played for Villa between 1991 and 1994.

Charles N'Zogbia
played for the club between 2011 and 2016, making 93 appearances.

Zat Knight
was a centre-back who played for the Villa from 2007-2009.

THE BEST OF THE REDS

THE LIVERPOOL A-Z

www.g2books.co.uk

THE BEST OF THE GERS

THE RANGERS A-Z

RANGERS
FOOTBALL CLUB
150
ANNIVERSARY
1872 · 2022

By Graham Betts and Rob Mason

www.g2books.co.uk

SUPER JACK

THE JACK GREALISH STORY
BRITAIN'S FIRST £100 MILLION PLAYER
Written by Simon Goodyear

www.g2books.co.uk